Contents

"My sister said you used to be strict"

Mike Priestley

Published in the United Kingdom by

Michael G Priestley Books

Content copyright © Michael G Priestley, 2024.

A CIP record of this book is available from the British Library.

First printed 2024.

Layout and design by Unwin Print, Farnsfield, Newark, Nott's. NG22 8JN.

ISBN 9780957413474

1. Grammar-Gog

I just fell into teaching. I had not been a particularly good pupil. I was rather lazy and I had a short attention span. I found it difficult throughout my school days to sit still for more than half an hour at a time. My legs would start twitching (they still do) and I was just desperate to get out on my bike or down to the park. At school, I was a day-dreamer, frequently drifting off into my own world until a direct question from the front abruptly interrupted my imagination and jolted me back into the here and now.

With the unstinting love and support of my adoptive parents, I was very happy at home and I soon learnt how to put off any uncomfortable decisions that might otherwise have disturbed my equilibrium. I created extra holiday time for myself by feigning illness, especially in the first couple of years at big school, though that pattern had actually begun a year earlier, as is recorded in my surviving junior school reports. I think that I probably preferred to be at home in my room for much of the time, with my train set, comics and music.

My memories of primary school are few. I attended four different ones, largely because we moved house to a different part of town half way through that stage, in December 1956, when I was seven years old. I had an unfortunate start in the early days at my infant school. I let flow what turned out to be a very productive wee in my shorts, whilst sitting on the hall floor during an assembly. I categorically denied being the perpetrator, as the pool in which I was the only island gradually seeped outwards in all directions across the polished wooden surface. Those parked all around me gradually inched away, making their accusations as they went. "It wasn't me", I insisted, though the evidence to the contrary was irrefutable.

The pictures in Mum's old family album show us all in neck to calf-length smocks for our formal 1954 class photos, taken both indoors and out. They look like they were made out of old curtain material, with a range of different patterns on view across the group. I think we must have all been told not to smile for the camera, too, though the next shot from a page or two further on in Mum's collection suggests that instruction had been discarded by the following year - as, thankfully, had the overall garments themselves.

A brief school report for July 1957 indicates that my conduct was *"Normal - Chatters"*, which, shows, at least, that I was probably getting on OK with my peers. This was followed a year later with the observation that he (I) should *"guard against trying to finish his work quickly as this makes him very careless"*.

The last two years at primary school were all about preparation for the eleven plus exam. This meant concentrating on English, maths and what were perhaps best described as exercises in logic. It was all very regimented, and practice tests were addressed with some regularity. There were forty-five of us in our top class, and when it came to the real thing, we all got through safely. This was largely because we had all been selected already by the age of nine as those candidates within the year group most likely to succeed, and we were drilled thereafter with that goal in mind. I believe that we were also put in the hands of the teacher specially entrusted to produce the right results for us and for the reputation of the school. At times, we were even sorted into the seating order which reflected our performance in the internal practice tests. I was nineteenth in one such test and for a time I shared a double desk with the boy who came twentieth. I think its fair to say that we had a pretty good idea where we stood in the intellectual pecking order from about nine onwards. Maybe even that is a bit disingenuous, as I think children probably realise very early on that some of their peers are obviously cleverer than they are and that others are not.

Looking for a bit of light relief at home from all this pressure, I can't quite remember exactly when it was that I graduated from Children's Favourites with Uncle Mac to the hit parade on Radio Luxembourg, but it was certainly in time for both "Johnny Remember Me" by John Leyton and Johnny Tillotson with "Poetry in Motion", which was a little earlier still. The switch soon led to the acquisition - with my parents' help - of my own record player and a collection of vinyl "singles".

Having finally arrived at the grammar school, I soon decided that staying at home on my own again was so much easier than having to deal with people all day. It was not because I was being bullied at school. As a regular park footballer already, I was savvy enough to get by most of the time in the company of a group of friends. I usually managed to handle the nasties in the playground and elsewhere by deflection or attempts at humour, so it was not that I was particularly afraid of going to school. I just don't think that I can have liked it there very much.

Taking extra time off did cost me, though. I was demoted after the end of year exams at age twelve into the

"C" class, which was clearly the sort of blow to one's self-esteem that could have contributed to greater lethargy and disinterest later on, though I had no-one to blame but myself. Without any apparent personal drive or any budding signs of ambition, I just ticked over until I was too old to go to school any more, by which time I was nineteen.

In passing the eleven plus exam, I had been accepted by my first-choice school, the same grammar school that my father had so proudly attended as a scholarship boy in the 1920s. I failed most of the "O" levels in the courses that I followed from age fourteen to sixteen. Had I chosen art, which would have been my instinctive choice, instead of trying to please Dad by taking on Latin, I would have sailed seamlessly into the sixth form with the required four passes needed to progress to "A" levels. Instead, I wasted a further year, languishing in what was amusingly called "remove", a sort of half-way staging post between the fifth-form and the sixth - a kind of holding bay for those that they did not really know what to do with.

Most of the inmates in there did not know what to do with themselves, either. It was an arena characterised by aimlessness. Perhaps the school had demonstrated in their choice of a name for it, what they actually thought of its incumbents. More precisely, the term had its derivation deep in the public-school system of the past. They were probably only too pleased to have had an opportunity to resurrect it for that reason alone. In an appropriate - though presumably unintended - act of symbolism, remove's classroom was positioned in a tiny annexe to the main building next to the separate toilet block. When the classroom door was left open on warm days, the unmistakeable aroma from the loos wafted our way and as far as what should have been my seat of learning.

Those toilets were detached from the main building, though connected to it by a covered walkway that also provided an entrance to the central part of the school via a short flight of steps. The bogs, as we called them, were cold and draughty in winter but at least they were adjacent to the main building. The junior school equivalent had been at the bottom of the playground, so sometimes you had to tramp across the snow or run through the rain to reach them. Once there, we amused ourselves by seeing how far up the wall above the trough we could fire a jet of urine. That was one of the few things I remember being really good at during my time in the upper juniors. It would almost certainly have been enough to get me another caning.

The year before I had landed in remove, an enterprising member of the class had won privileges from the headmaster - in an uncharacteristically radical move - which allowed the boys to be treated, on paper at least, like the others of their age who had already moved on to the sixth form proper.

Very little learning took place in remove. I remember a geography teacher who liked to give us something to do that involved a lot of writing. He then put his feet up on his desk and read the Guardian newspaper. It was certainly liberal for him, but hardly progressive for us. A linguist gave up trying to teach us altogether after receiving a less than enthusiastic response to his instructions and on one occasion he even went to lie down across a row of chairs at the back of the room and feigned going to sleep, in protest at the lack of cooperation he had been afforded.

Nor was he the only one that could not wait to get to bed. Once a week, our class had a library lesson overseen by the long-standing deputy-head who was approaching retirement. The quiet session he was able to cultivate on the basis of his reputation as a disciplinarian also meant that he was able to nod off himself during the first session after lunch in the padded armchair behind his desk. He was usually woken by his own snoring as his head suddenly lolled forward, and before we had had a chance to raise so much as a titter.

Serious card games were played for money, and undertaken in the back corner of the classroom during those lessons where it was considered no fuss would ensue from the front. Some masters who sought the quiet life turned a blind eye to it. When we were let out from our den to wander as far as the science laboratory, some lads would entertain themselves by lobbing the house bricks - which were being used as make-shift Bunsen burner stands - across the classroom to each other, while the teacher was facing the blackboard. Rule One, I decided at a later date, was that as a teacher, you should never turn your back on the class for more than a second.

I spent many hours gazing across the river from that upstairs physics lab' at the trails of steam left behind by passenger trains, about a mile away from my bench, as they threaded their way outwards through the docklands on the series of viaducts leading from the terminus station in the city centre. That was probably just one of the reasons that I scored only 3% in my "O" level preliminary exam and I was told not to bother taking the real thing later in the year.

The laboratories always stank of gas when our class was in there, as boys constantly fiddled with the gas taps throughout the sessions. Other more daring individuals randomly splattered ink from their fountain pens down the backs of the masters' black gowns, as they prowled the aisles between the rows of desks, during yet more tedious note copying sessions.

When musing over it during the years that followed, I concluded that the school authorities would have preferred it if my classmates and I had already left the school at sixteen. I felt we were now just an embarrassment to them in this supposedly privileged, selective environment, the notion of which the school cherished so much.

The whole year was partially rescued for me by two splendid, youthful and inspiring teachers, one of history and one of English, both of whom - quite surprisingly, as it must have appeared at the time, because it was not what we were used to in the rest of our lessons - made realistic efforts to engage with the class on a proper basis. In more modern parlance and for much of the rest of the time, our needs were most definitely not being met.

I managed to scrape together a couple more "O" level passes while passing through remove, sufficient to allow me belated access to the sixth form the following year, including a re-sit of geography, which I would amazingly end up teaching. I was probably the only geography teacher ever to have previously failed the subject at "O" level. It is also likely that there were not that many people who had failed it with a grade seven in the summer and had then gone on to achieve a grade one a few months afterwards, either.

I didn't do much better in the sixth form when I finally got there. Any lingering affection I had for my old school probably drained away during that time. I was sent home from school out of the blue one day to get a hair-cut. My hair had grown sufficiently long for it to be touching my collar, which was apparently the millimetre or two that made all the difference between acceptability and falling standards during the Beatles era.

Interest in my head (other than for strictly cerebral purposes) was maintained into the upper-sixth, too, when, as an eighteen-year-old young man, I was assaulted by the head of history. It was during a private study period in the library. Now occupying a brand-new building, we were seated in individual booths with wooden partitions, presumably designed to discourage unnecessary communication with other pupils. I had probably carried on talking after silence had been demanded, or, more likely, I had just laughed out loud at someone else's comment. The teacher approached me from behind and smacked me forcibly across the back of the head. I had not seen him coming. I don't remember much being said immediately afterwards by either of us, so from his point of view it probably had the impact (literally) that he was looking for. This long-serving member of staff knew my dad and that evening I told my folks what had happened. However, without any need for prompting, the head of history unreservedly apologised to my parents by phone. Maybe he feared repercussions or perhaps he just regretted it. It reinforced my belief that using a position of authority to assault children (and young men) was not just unacceptable as a means of correction but was simply wrong.

What was my sixth form attendance leading towards, anyway? It would be something on the railways, of course, because that was my main hobby and prime interest, and wouldn't it be nice to have a hobby for life and get paid for it. An interview was looming, at Euston House, Eversholt Street in London, for entry into the British Railway's Management Training Scheme. I was told that success depended on my gaining any two "A" level passes, and so, shortly before the exams themselves and because I was never one for taking on more than was strictly necessary, I jettisoned history, which I had discovered a liking for and was actually quite good at, on the grounds that I would certainly pass general studies without having to revise for it - except, of course, that I failed it. It must have been the science bit that let me down, or it could have been the foreign languages section, or, I had to admit, perhaps it was the literature……

I finally left school a year later than most of my contemporaries. I viewed the experience with a range of emotions. I had initially been so gleeful to have passed the eleven plus exam, on which, I had been told by so many, that so much would hinge later on. I enjoyed the railway society film shows and the trips to various railway locations immensely, and I was grateful to those teachers who gave up whole days in their holidays to take us on our railway-related jaunts.

As a good friend recently reminded me, we also have the grammar school to thank for the opportunity to meet up with each other. Four of us came together as a close-knit group in 1960 and with a younger brother and further additions from the technical grammar school, the nearest

Catholic grammar school and one from park football, we can now celebrate over sixty years of continuous friendship. For that, above all else school days related, I am exceedingly grateful.

I had initially been quite proud to be a grammar school boy because it instantly conferred a feeling of superiority over those who had failed it. By the time I left, I could see how damaging the whole regime had been, unhealthily splitting up friendship groups and families and labelling them as successes and failures when they were still in short trousers. Most of my junior school friends passed, too, so we had all trotted off to one or other of the two boys' grammar schools in the town - except one, who failed and who would normally have gone to the secondary modern school. In middle-class areas like ours, however, parents who saw that coming would often send their children to private school rather than face the ignominy of having their child stand out like a sore thumb in our leafy and comparatively privileged part of town. On the streets, it had created a divide that would have been more noticeable had we not been compulsive park footballers. We kept in touch with many of the lads whom we might otherwise have consistently dismissed thereafter as "scallies", when, at the same time, we had suddenly become "grammar-gogs".

I had also discovered that selection did not end at eleven. I thought that the grammar school consistently concentrated its efforts on clever, well-motivated boys and those who excelled at rugby football and cricket. Sports day was also a major event involving the whole school in one capacity or other, and leading to the presentation of a trophy to the victor ludorum, as the most successful athlete overall. Some of these young men came across to me as very self-satisfied and disdainful. There was a lot of swaggering going on. We were growing up in a very competitive environment, in which they were constantly being feted for their successes. I felt that the rest of us were somehow just providing an audience - the backdrop for their triumphs.

During our first year there, we had a slightly wider curriculum that would then narrow as time progressed. We all sampled woodwork, for example, where the master in charge enjoyed damning us with faint praise. "You are the cream of the town", he yelled, meaning that that was the description that we were actually failing to live up to. His outburst was accompanied by the jettisoning of someone's inadequate wooden teapot stand, complete with bevelled edges and mortice and tenon joint, to the far end of the workshop, in disgust. It was a typically strange mixture of assumed superiority and simultaneous humiliation. I often wondered how the art, woodwork and physical education teachers felt on school photo days as the only teachers not wearing academic gowns.

Even the prefects had gowns - sixth formers visibly marked out already as the next generation's movers and shakers. Those pupils chosen as potential university material were also awarded striped blazers and prefects' badges and encouraged to get used to ordering people about by taking an active part in the "fagging" system. This meant that they could legitimately make various requests of boys who were in their first year at the school, who then had to perform menial tasks on their behalf. In practice, this would usually mean various "fetching and carrying" errands that were generally food related. They even had the right to detain anyone who disobeyed their instructions.

Those in their first year at the school were also subjected to bouts of "coshing". This involved being assaulted by boys who had been there a whole year already. They would roll up and knot their cloth handkerchiefs (affectionately referred to as "snot rags"), maybe wetting them or adding a bit of sand from the long jump pit to the knotted end. They then went around hitting the newcomers over the head with them. As we had to wear caps in "the fags", the assailants would approach you from behind, whip off your headgear with one hand and then whack you over the head with the cosh wielded in the other one. This was generally interpreted as fair game - just another jolly jape pinched, no doubt, from the public schools, where there were almost certainly even more unpleasant initiation ceremonies being undertaken. The fact was that this was condoned by the staff by their inaction in making any attempt to stamp it out. I imagine they saw it as a justifiable part of a "toughening up" process. I can't think that it would have done any good at all to complain about being on the receiving end, however aggressive it might have become.

It was not generally a good idea to claim to be enjoying a birthday, either, because that would mean being subjected to the "bumps". That involved your companions employing anyone else who happened to be passing at the time to grab an arm or a leg, pull you to the ground then repeatedly lift you as high in the air as possible before dumping you rather unceremoniously back to earth, with little regard for vertebrae.

A friend from that time reminded me that on one occasion that there was a serious fight going on between two boys in the yard, as the playground was sometimes referred to, when the physical education teacher suddenly turned up. Instead of stopping proceedings and trying to get to the bottom of the incident that had led to violence, he marched them both off to the gym, equipped them with boxing gloves and encouraged them to carry on hitting each other. Suffice it to say, that it would probably be a dismissible offence today.

Much more unsavoury than all of these as a playground pastime was the treatment of the one known pupil who was gay, though that word was not common parlance at that time, in that way. An overweight, older boy, he habitually spent break times clinging to his satchel with his arms folded in front of him (to physically protect himself, presumably) and leaning with his back to the wall, literally as well as metaphorically, whilst certain protagonists picked on smaller boys and threw them towards him as some kind of sacrificial offering. Had this been an isolated incident, I may not even have recalled it, but it was not. It was par for the course and at a time that homosexuality was still an offence. As a clear example of sustained bullying alone, I don't remember ever hearing that it had been brought up as an issue of concern, never mind being dealt with. One can only imagine what torment that young man had to endure on a daily basis. His demeanour throughout was one of resigned acceptance. He tried to smile so as not to attract further unwanted attention, but what must he have really been thinking on his way to school each day?

Back in class, note taking regularly included copying sections from books but also might be in the form of dictation. I had won a Sunday school prize for my italic handwriting in my last year at junior school but writing in italics under these changed circumstances was always going to be a massive challenge. We were now having to write twice as fast from the moment we started at the grammar school. My carefully formed letters, fashioned from my Osmiroid fountain pen with its slightly angled nib and filled with royal blue Quink ink, did not have a hope of keeping up. If the ink ran out half-way through the piece, then I was completely stuffed. My writing became an untidy scrawl as I struggled to keep pace.

Grammar schools, of course, are not yet a thing of the past. They are allowed to cling on in some parts of the country which the radical changes towards comprehensive schooling did not reach in the 1960s and 1970s. Indeed, in her 2017 election manifesto, the Prime Minister, Theresa May, sought to breathe new life into them, though her schemes were soon dropped as other more pressing issues assumed greater immediate importance for her political survival. *"We will build a better Britain not just for the privileged few"*, Mrs May had said in her first speech as Prime Minister. What could fly in the face of her stated intention more obviously than the resurrection of an education system that was past its sell-by date in the 1960s and which, by design, catered primarily and specifically for the "privileged few"?

You could just about argue up until the 1960s that a management class needed treating differently from those who were destined for the mass-employment, heavy industries of the past (coal mining, ship building, steel making, dock labouring, textiles, railways, etc). In our lifetime, however, the industrial landscape has been transformed by globalisation and deindustrialisation and the requirements of our education system are now substantially different, the prime example being a universal requirement to keep up with the revolution in communications technology.

Far from providing a vehicle for disadvantaged pupils to excel, grammar schools perpetuated the advantages of the middle-class. Our grammar school was full of middle-class kids. Anecdotally, I would suspect that working-class kids were but a small and a generally less successful minority. Many former grammar school pupils remember the best days of their lives in a system which purposefully lauded them to such a degree that they eulogise about it to this day. They see it as encapsulating everything that was good about the good old days. They also seem to regard it now as some kind of panacea for everything that has gone wrong with society since. Their views are anachronistic. We have to try to make educational success a reality for all, not just the privileged few.

The term "bring-backery", which that move in 2017 typified, describes a nostalgic inclination to resurrect selected practices from a somewhat rose-tinted past. As a principle of government, it is not a good idea. Things have been jettisoned for a reason. I prefer to keep faith with the optimistic notion that mankind makes changes which generally turn out to be for the better.

Grammar schools perpetuated and entrenched advantages already enjoyed by sections of the community, in spite of the fact that some of them had initially been set up as charitable institutions to help the poor. Far from encouraging social mobility, they ended up hindering it. Evidence suggests that areas with grammar schools do not perform better than those that have gone comprehensive, when the results from grammar and other secondary schools in the same authority are added together. More recent flag-bearers may have been the comparatively successful products of that system but they got there at the expense of the majority who received a second-class education as a result. If you choose to select, you must also choose to reject at the same time.

On occasions throughout my life, I have met people who have sounded quite impressed when they have learnt that I was grammar school educated. Usually, they did not go to one themselves. They had allowed themselves to become seduced by a mystique that was way beyond the reality. My experiences there did not justify any such assumptions. As can be seen, I was not perhaps the typical grammar school boy, but neither was I by any means the only failure within that system. However, I think my relative failure gave me the opportunity to stand back and analyse what I went through more objectively, rather than being swept along on the tide of acclaim that the top pupils enjoyed.

As I flicked through the written evidence from my time there in the form of my school reports, I noticed the occasions that I had actually performed quite well in some subjects. This would have been on the basis of very little real effort. I did not do any meaningful revision for exams until I was in the sixth form and only managed it spasmodically even then. That must have been apparent to my subject teachers at the time, yet I don't remember anyone ever pulling me aside and saying "What are you playing at? This result shows both of us what you are capable of. Well done - now why don't you build on that?" I would have required that "word in the ear" sort of encouragement to have changed my attitude. I don't believe that it ever came my way at secondary school. Formality at a distance was the established order, so "Pull your socks up, lad!"

Luckily for me, success at school did not seem to matter much if you wanted to be a teacher in 1968. They were desperate for them. It was very much a result of the principle of supply and demand, much as it always has been. New technology colleges and universities to fill, the move from selective to comprehensive education to cater for, the building of new schools for recently developed estates that were replacing decrepit inner-city areas undergoing slum clearance programmes, meeting the continuing requirements of an extended baby boom generation, preparing to extend the period of compulsory education to sixteen years of age and encouraging a greater take up of sixth form places, all probably worked in my favour.

I thought that one or two of the prospective teachers who turned up for interview on the same day as me were not necessarily exactly what they were looking for. Even I could see that and I wasn't too sure that I wanted to do it myself. The lecturer on the panel who quizzed me, a little late in the day, once my plans for sorting out the railway network had dissolved and I was flailing around for alternatives, said that I must have something about me if I could get a grade "A" at "A" level in geography, even though that was actually all that I had achieved as a sixth-former. I comforted myself with the thought that I was probably also in a pretty select band of students who had initially failed "O" level in that subject and had, nevertheless, gone on to get an "A" at the higher level.

It was amazing what a burst of proper studying could lead to if you set your mind to it, I thought, rather surprising myself into the bargain. I was actually very proud of my "A". It indicated to me what I might be capable of if I ever decided to concentrate my efforts on "getting on". I had also shown some of the grammar school staff that they had consistently under-estimated me. Even the sixth form geography teacher, who I liked and respected, had only put me down for a "C". In the end, that master felt obliged to give me the annual geography prize, given that the other two major successes in the subject were both potential Oxbridge highfliers who had been expressed into the fifth form a year early and were therefore two years younger than me at the time that we all sat the exams. They were already much more mature than me in every possible way. They were also used to being showered with prizes from all angles, so my "A" effectively gave the staff an opportunity to spread things about a bit more. I chose a book of photographs of steam locomotives called "Castles and Kings" and never regretted it for a moment. It is still on my shelf all these years later, though it smells a bit musty now, when I leaf through it.

I did not go to teacher training college to learn to teach. I went there to give myself some more breathing space, as if I had not had enough of that already. Three more years without actually having to make a final decision about a career was how I saw it. I received a grant, too. They were actually going to give me money for a full three years, in spite of the fact that I came from a reasonably comfortably middle-class background. Brilliant, I thought.

I would still be living at home, thus saving even more cash for myself, though anyone else could have seen that I was making another big mistake on the growing up front. It was a lovely cushy existence. A further two hours were wasted commuting each day, but I liked travelling, just watching the world go by. I timed my working day, to stretch that concept a shade further, around my own personal requirements. Top of the list was a businessmen's lunch, as near as daily as I could fix it. It was half a crown - two shillings and sixpence - for a massive roast chicken dinner in the basement dining rooms somewhere near to one of the main line railway stations in the central business district in the city. Additionally, I always enjoyed a chocolate bar on the way home on the train, contributing steadily, no doubt, to the numerous fillings which have greeted me during the decades that have followed, every time subsequently that I have opened my mouth to brush my teeth. The imperative to build the day around food meant that even with a very early or a very late lunch, I had to choose which was the most important section of the college day, morning or afternoon, and then frequently turn down the invitation to tutorials, lectures and seminars that inevitably often fell into an inconvenient time slot, as far as my dinner date with myself was concerned.

I had no responsibilities. The work was easy. It was like doing "A" levels again, only over a wider range of subjects, including geology, educational theory and American studies, though it was probably even less demanding intellectually. Some of the courses were really weak and lacking in any meaningful challenge, being heavily descriptive in design, though I thought that the subject matter was usually quite interesting, even if I was not intending to do a great deal with it. I was faced with the choice of either doing things properly or drifting along, as before. Unsurprisingly, I chose drifting along again. I sat upstairs on the bus out to college on the city outskirts and watched the citizens going about their very much more purposeful business, and then I came back into the centre after my truncated college day along a different route, just for a change of scene.

The only uncomfortable bit started when they thought it might be a good idea for me to try doing some teaching. I did not particularly relish this idea. I was being put on the spot in a way that I was not used to. I was sent to a series of middle schools, relatively new inventions in Britain at that time, which had allowed local authorities to go comprehensive less painfully by making more complete use of the existing buildings. They were a pragmatic response to the financial demands that the reform had imposed. Some lecturers tried to persuade the students otherwise, insisting there were good pedagogical reasons for moving kids around more often than they needed to during their school lives, but I thought that was unlikely.

I discovered an important fact about education through that set up, though. Adopting a new "good idea" that is in vogue, for whatever reason, can be a very handy way to get on in education, if you are that way inclined. You then choose to be a proponent, cobble up some justification including the adoption of a bit of handy jargon, try to get a bit of backing from people who are themselves "known", even if only in a parochial way and their support is tentative and lukewarm. Now you have become a self-appointed "expert" on the topic. Then you write a book or even just a paper and get it published in the educational press. Following that, you address groups of impressionable colleagues and get promotion on the strength of your "achievements". You move on, someone fills your previous position and makes their name by - you have guessed it - advocating a change and almost certainly one that involves dismantling your own initiative.

By this time, my three years of general and gentle hedonism were up - three years without alcohol (I was teetotal until I was twenty-three, though I did make up for that somewhat thereafter), without drugs (I was too apprehensive to dabble and I never have since) and with relatively few cigarettes (I bought them infrequently. I probably cadged more from others than I purchased myself, and I gave them up altogether when I was twenty-two, after losing a badminton match and casting round for something to blame other than my own poor play).

I had still not come up with a more attractive alternative to teaching, so it looked like I would have to give it a go. I applied for a job with my own local authority and the one next door. I was knocked back by my own home town after an undistinguished interview. It had a posher image than its more industrial neighbour and was therefore a more desirable place to teach, but there were consequently more people chasing fewer posts. I was going to have to settle for a bit of a journey to work. I bought a second-hand moped to complete this commute, which a new colleague was instantly and dismissively to describe as "a hair dryer on wheels".

The interview in my second-choice local authority had only lasted a matter of minutes. I was asked what my subject was. The solitary and over-wrought town hall pen-pusher on the other side of the enormous oak desk used his ruler to manoeuvre his way around an extremely large piece of paper, which had what looked like a matrix inscribed on it. When his y axis and his x axis were aligned to his satisfaction, he looked up at me for the first time, told me the name of my destination and added, *"Start in September"*. That was it. *"Thank you very much"*, I replied, followed by *"Goodbye"*, as the interviewer got to his feet.

I knew a bit about the place that had been specified. It was a sprawling out of town council housing estate, built to replace the old inner-urban terraces. It had a reputation for being really rough. I returned to college feeling a little dazed. What the hell have I done? I thought. My tutor smiled on hearing the news. *"That's good"*, he said, adding, *"If you survive there you will survive anywhere"*. I was going to be a teacher. I amazed myself further by turning up in September on day one, as requested.

I had not covered myself in glory as a pupil and a student, but I may just have stumbled across some important lessons about the nature of ambition, potential, motivation, inspiration and the under-estimation of ability along the way. Beginning to think about such issues a bit more carefully would possibly help me later on. Having come from a fairly privileged background and certainly one that was above average for the times in all sorts of ways, and having not made full use of the opportunities presented to me so far by any stretch of the imagination, I had yet to learn just how lucky I had been. Now I was going to have to sink or swim, which was a shame because swimming was yet another uncomfortable challenge that I had not yet got around to tackling.

2. Call Yourself a Teacher?

My career as a classroom teacher began. It was then described as an assistant teacher's role to separate it from those with responsibility for a department. I ended up staying at my first school in that capacity for eleven years. The school was undoubtedly "on the way up" throughout that time. Two former and adjacent secondary modern schools, boys and girls, had been physically connected by passageways on two levels to create a new mixed comprehensive school. Though it was primarily a neighbourhood school with a very working-class catchment area in a post-war, out of town council housing estate, it also served sizeable suburban, owner-occupier districts in two relatively middle-class enclaves that were a bit further afield.

At a later stage, when overall pupil numbers were just starting to fall, one of these settlements was removed from the school's feeder system. The belief was that this enabled the grammar schools - in what had been the neighbouring council's patch before local government reorganisation - to keep their numbers up, or at least to avoid having to water down their selective intake too much. It appeared to be a decision to benefit the privileged few in a nearby area to the detriment of our school. Welcome to education politics, I might reasonably have thought. That would become an important part of my future working life, though I did not know it at the time.

It was exciting to be associated with an improving school. There was a large and lively staff already in place, with a mixture of experienced graduates from grammar school backgrounds in the old town centre added to the pre-existing secondary modern staff, who were already on the site. The third component - an injection of "new blood" - was to include me. I started to accept some responsibility for myself for the first time. I did not want to fail, though I had to fight my way back after a weak start. Fighting back, in itself, was a new concept to me. Initially, I thought that I could befriend the lads I was to teach. After all, I was still playing football with youngsters like them every night after school that daylight would allow it. Not so - it was not the same. I was very naïve. They did not want my friendship, I was soon to discover, but they were prepared to respect me on another level, once I had got my priorities sorted out. I gradually got things right, but it took longer than it should have done. I had a lingering thought that I should have moved on after a year or two and started again, and if I had been career minded that is precisely what I would have done. I was not adventurous or ambitious enough to do it at that stage.

My first year in teaching coincided with preparations for the raising of the school leaving age from fifteen to sixteen, which became known as Rosla and was due to start in the following September. The old stagers were panicking. What were they going to do with them for the extra year? I volunteered for the curriculum development working party. New courses were devised, areas which might at a later date have been assigned to the domains of personal and social education, social studies, citizenship or integrated humanities, none of which existed at that time. There was a considerable reluctance to break out from the disciplinary straight-jacket provided by the traditional subject boundaries, or to provide any classroom opportunities to discuss controversial but relevant issues of the day - things that would be taken for granted as necessary parts of the curriculum in one form or another in years to come. Topics like contraception, health and hygiene, civil rights, the emancipation of women, participatory democracy, family budgeting and crime and punishment would all eventually find their niche as timetable subject matter in one form or another.

It is an irony that the biggest problem then was what to do with the less academic senior pupils, and that would still be one of the biggest challenges in schools when I finally left the profession. Some circumstances changed very dramatically over that forty years and all kinds of educational diets were tried and then passed over along the way.

I quickly developed an interest in trying to improve what was on offer. Within my subject, I met representatives of the examination system known as Geography for the Young School Leaver, who had come in to school to see my head of department to try to persuade him to change the way that geography was delivered at the fourteen to sixteen-year-old assessment level, at least for the less able students. My immediate boss was not impressed. He was a hard-working and well-meaning man, but not at all progressive. He had been at the boys' secondary modern school previously and was mainly concerned with developing the more academic side of things. Although he was a good teacher himself at all levels, he was not going to take any risks. I found this reluctance to take up new initiatives rather frustrating.

For a time, I turned my energies instead to considering my own advancement. I felt under-qualified, compared to the graduate staff. This was hardly surprising, as I had spent most of my existence up to that time amusing myself, and without demonstrating much in the way of self-discipline. I went about improving matters. I took and passed the general paper and geology at "O" level, then gained a second grade "A" at "A" level, somewhat belatedly, in history. I completed an Open University degree in social science and eventually got seconded for a further year of full-time study at college. This time around, I took it more seriously, and as a result I turned my recently acquired graduate status into a First-Class B. Ed. Honours degree. I was catching up, at last. I now had eight "O" levels, two "A" levels and a fairly good degree, like many of my colleagues. I no longer felt different, in that respect. I had only reached the level that I knew I should have achieved in the first place. I did not doubt that I could do it, but previously it had not meant enough to me to try. I was gradually becoming more focussed. I now knew that I wanted to make a measurable contribution to things, even if in a small way. To do that, I knew that I would have to become a departmental head.

In those days, managers of subjects had considerable influence over what exam courses were followed, what type of geography was taught and how it was delivered. My head of department was a lifer. He did not want to move, either upwards or to another school. I could not stay there and expect to be promoted. I could have waited for other local opportunities to arise, but it could have taken ages until something suitable had come up and even then, there was no guarantee that I would be successful with my application. My first school head was very good to me. I had been promoted to the position of head of year, which was a bit of a sinecure in this instance, though that was definitely not the case everywhere else, as I was to discover. Here, it enabled the head to reward people that he could see were trying hard. It involved taking a year assembly once a week (in order for the head to satisfy national directives for regular joint worship) and the acquisition of a bit of extra status and that was about all.

However, there was a positive vibe about the place all the time that I was there and staff student relationships were generally good. A lot of people put in a lot of hard work and results steadily improved. A sixth form was gradually built up where there had not been one before and many of the senior pupils aspired to be part of it. The largely youthful, talented and energetic staff involved themselves in a range of extra-curricular activities, including staff football matches and school trips abroad - both of which I contributed to - as well as some elaborate and extravagant musical and drama productions to entertain and, indeed, to help to weld the school community at large. I got stuck into them, too.

Becoming properly qualified, if somewhat belatedly, increased my confidence and I knew that I was ready to take on greater responsibility. It still surprised me, nevertheless, that in all the time that I spent there, I was never formally inspected, nor even had to share my teaching room for a minute with an outsider at all and only very fleetingly and never formally with my head of department, a deputy or any other member of staff. I could not remember the head ever coming to my teaching room, even when he was showing visitors round the school. At first, I had found this rather bewildering. "Do you mean I just get on with it in my own way? Isn't anybody going to check that I'm doing things properly?" I concluded that this was what it meant to be a trusted professional - you worked as hard as you wanted to, you had complete freedom to decide how you operated and as long as you had your head of department's approval you could more or less choose what you wanted to do in the first place. It is great credit to the people who worked there at that time that such good progress was made to develop the school in the way that transpired.

Good relationships with the pupils and the wider community were forged at a time when circumstances and the environment outside the school in the catchment area were becoming increasingly difficult for its residents. In short, the whole region was already in quite dramatic economic decline. The traditional industries in the town were on the wane. The biggest local private industry employer suddenly substantially reduced the number of students that they had previously taken each year on apprenticeships. These had been coveted prizes amongst the town's young people. Then they stopped them altogether. Unemployment rose. The urban fabric declined. The reputation of the estate where the school was situated deteriorated further. Increasingly, it became better known as a centre for social problems, disaffection and especially for drug abuse.

The school had its fair share of problem family "names," but they were identified and contained during my time there and they never consistently set the agenda for everyone else. Everybody felt the difficult few were the anti-social odd ones out. Suspensions and expulsions were relatively rare.

However, other things were changing, too. As a staff, we were obliged, as I understood it, to respond to a directive from the European Court of Human Rights relating to corporal punishment. Caning kids as a punishment for a wide range of misdeeds was commonplace and widely accepted as necessary to keep discipline in schools at that time. I had been caned three times whilst I was at junior school (though never at secondary school) and all for very minor transgressions, including talking in assembly and being in the wrong part of the yard during playtime (there was an invisible line on the tarmac that separated us from the seniors). Each time, it had been three strokes across the palm of the hand and it stung like mad afterwards. Thinking back, it was the same teacher on each occasion, someone I otherwise had no contact with during any normal school day. Every time I had come across him it was to receive a punishment, it seemed. He was just a classroom teacher for another class. He had no additional role for maintaining discipline that I was aware of. One wonders how he spent the rest of his day when I was not around. The suspicion was, of course, that some folk quite enjoyed doing that sort of thing to children.

A vote was taken on the issue during a staff meeting. I was the only one out of about seventy staff to vote for its abolition. I would have done the same at any stage of my career, before or since, though I had to admit that the relatively straightforward time that I had enjoyed in the classroom up to that point, was, to an extent, based on the fear that many of the pupils had for the cane, which was wielded (officially, anyway) by senior staff rather than by classroom teachers, but on whose authority I depended, and indeed had to turn to from time to time in my early days. It helped control the majority, who had to think before they acted - should I or should I not take part in this bit of nonsense? It had a sobering effect on most people, just as it had done at my own grammar school, when I was there as a pupil a decade beforehand.

There were also a very few tough, un-cooperative figures in the school who were not afraid of the cane. Those that were used to violence in their everyday lives were untroubled by the prospect of a bit more of it. They were feared by their peers and no doubt by many of the teaching staff as well. Strangely, they did not always take advantage of their notoriety whilst they were in the building, preferring, no doubt, to save their energies for more earnest mayhem around the town outside of school hours. Instead, they gave the impression of coming to school for a rest between feverish periods of anti-social activity elsewhere. By and large, I discovered that one could usually jolly them along, making sure one did not aggravate them by insisting they work any harder than they felt they wanted to, or by being too obsessive about their adherence to every single aspect of the school's rule book, including minor infringements of the uniform regulations. Some of them were very moody and a very few were hard-faced liars - appearing to me at the time to exude real menace. They concentrated their day time activities around a lot of intimidating posturing. I tried to keep eye contact with such souls to a minimum. Everybody knew who they were. There was an uneasy co-existence, which boiled over every now and then in odd instances, like the day it was rumoured that they had beaten up the assistant caretaker, but, perhaps unsurprisingly, things like that were hushed up as much as possible. Those individuals never really threatened the way the school was run for the benefit of everyone else, on a day-to-day basis.

On one occasion, a known trouble-maker emerged mid-way through a session from a room at the end of the corridor near my classroom, and so I asked the boy why he was out of his lesson. *"Got stabbed in art"* was his relatively nonchalant reply, given the circumstances. He pulled up the front of his blazer to show me the patch of blood seeping through his light blue shirt. A class-mate had stuck a pair of scissors into him below his rib cage and he was on the way to the office for some assistance. It could have had very serious consequences. Such occurrences were thankfully very rare.

There were some tough staff there too. Some used noise, bluster and threats to good effect, particularly in assembly and on the corridors. Some taught with their classroom door wide open so that everyone else could witness how strict they were. As a young assistant teacher, I felt reassured by the presence of colleagues who paraded themselves around the place in this way with a bit of over-inflated self-importance, which came over as "I am in charge and you had better believe it". Indeed, this style of behaviour typified the very specific role of a deputy head with responsibility for pastoral matters, though that particular description of the role was not commonly used at that time. There was a female deputy head of similar reputation, who dealt with the girls in the same manner. In their position of seniority, these dependable members of staff would have to deal with a fairly steady stream of naughty children sent to them by less assertive teachers and they would oblige by bellowing clichés at them without fear of contradiction. If that did not always work with a few of the harder cases, it certainly worked with most of the others and generally to the advantage of all. I always considered that the deputy heads' favourite members of staff must have been those who did not bring a regular trickle of troublesome pupils to see them. In fact, the ones they would admire most would have been those who never came to see them at all.

Nevertheless, the very specific role of the deputy heads helped create a framework of acceptable behaviour in which those teachers who found it difficult or impossible to do much shouting, or did not want to be involved in bellowing admonishment as a matter of course, could operate within a discipline system that they could imagine was their own, even though that was actually a bit of a mirage.

Not that this was the whole story, unfortunately, because one or two teachers that I had known over the years were bullies who took advantage of their position to administer whatever spontaneous "justice" they thought they could get away with. In some cases, that was quite a lot. They seemed to have a jokey, over-confident, overtly over-friendly relationship with some of the toughest kids, but the lads knew that this particular member of staff was quite assured in his own corner of the school, sufficient to take it upon themselves to humiliate them, with or without violence, if they saw the need to, which would almost always come in the form of a response to a perceived threat to their authority.

Meanwhile, I tried to set up my own stall based on reason, an energetic concern for my pupils' well-being, a youthful eagerness to get my subject across and a fairly dogged insistence on an acceptable level of behaviour. In practice, this meant firstly that when I wanted to speak to the class nobody else was allowed to talk and, secondly, I was determined that the classroom would be a quiet place in which people could get on and work without interruption from others. I claimed, with increasing confidence, that this was *not going to be a mess-about lesson*, a phrase I quite liked the sound of and therefore employed regularly for about the next twenty years or so, as we shall see. It was perfectly possible with most classes for me to set them off on a written task and then spend ten minutes chatting in the corridor to a colleague, who had established a similar working arrangement in an adjacent room. I did not go back to a riot, but possibly to a bit of murmuring and the turning of raised - rather than lowered - heads and the sort of order I wanted was quickly restored just by my being there again.

Children came to the school in what is now known as year eight (at age 12) and although the lower school classes could be irritatingly fidgety, they were generally well behaved. The more academic fourth and fifth formers (now years ten and eleven) were generally delightful and I found that I could usually encourage the less able senior pupils to make a bit of an effort, without too much hassle. I used to get a lot of *"Aar, eh, sir"* - good natured moaning in response to instructions to be followed or tasks to be addressed, but that was mostly as truculent as they got and most kids would have a go at the work, even if they found it boring or difficult. There was still an assumption at that time that children came to school to attempt the work that was put in front of them, without question. Teachers, the pupils and even their parents (by never questioning it, as for most it would have mirrored their own school experiences a generation earlier) generally adhered to this principle.

Given the state of some of the text books still in use and the lack of imagination and appeal that they contained, this was probably just as well. I gradually dispensed with many of them, but for years I had to admit that I relied too heavily instead on the hand-written output from the Banda machine, which produced A4 size worksheets and was fuelled by methylated spirit. Amazingly, it seemed to me when looking back, this had been something of a revolutionary new tool in itself. Its predecessor had been the Gestetner machine, also a drum-shaped printer, but electrically driven rather than hand operated like the Banda. It was less flexible because it relied on the previous and more time-consuming preparation of typed, foolscap-sized (taller than A4) master copies to duplicate information or question papers and which managed to successfully spread thick black ink just about everywhere else that one did not want it to go. The Banda gave teachers purple worksheets that stank of meth's and although staining was a little less of a problem, its main advantage was that it was portable. I made sure that I acquired one that I could call my own. It was placed on a shelf in my stock room and it was then put through a seriously rigorous and sustained test of its capabilities that lasted some years. Both means of duplication encouraged work that was far too repetitive and by modern comparisons hopelessly unattractive, but the students generally tended to get their heads down and do the business, because I had usually managed to pitch the work itself at the right level and make the tasks accessible for them.

If the grammar school had specialised in the copying of dictated notes and sections of prose out of text books, my first decade in teaching was, at least, something of an improvement, being the era of questioning. The justification was that old-fashion teaching methods relied on telling you stuff which you wrote down, learnt and then regurgitated during an exam. Perhaps because many of us had ourselves not long ago been on the receiving end of that prevalent pedagogy, and we had found it somewhat wanting, there was a definite shift in the 1970s towards trying to get pupils of all abilities to think for themselves a bit more. The two young teachers that I had had the good fortune to meet in my later years as a pupil in remove and the sixth-form were the first that I had come across who were that way inclined. It was all about posing appropriate questions, discussing possible responses and then fashioning distinctive, individual written answers. It was so much better than copying.

As far as geography was concerned it was soon clear that the syllabuses that were in place were enormous in terms of their scope. If you were going to have time to read, discuss, question and then provide answers, you were going to have to cut down on much of the bulk of the factual material that had been in there up to that point. This led to a clamour for syllabus change with a reduced content, in order to give teachers time to deal with the issues properly. That led, in turn, to counter-accusations from the establishment of the lowering of standards. I felt that as far as geography was concerned, teachers increasingly believed that they could no longer simply go right around the whole world writing descriptions of the Norwegian leather industry and every other economic activity in every country on the syllabus. They needed instead to choose the most appropriate examples of their type for whatever the topic in question was and concentrate on that. This would surely do away with unnecessary repetition. It was likely that history and some other subjects were probably faced with similar dilemmas at around the same time. They could not do all the British kings and queens there had ever been if they were going to find the necessary time to talk about them in a more inquisitive way. What about investigating their possible motives for the actions that they had taken, instead of just telling stories with dates presented as unquestionable facts?

By now, I fervently believed that curricular upheaval would lead to something better (and it did), but others saw it as the thin end of the wedge in a concerted nose-dive towards lower standards. They would describe the new interpretation of the subject as "butterfly geography", because, as they chose to interpret it, it flitted around here, there and everywhere in the search for meaningful examples, rather than attempting to cover everything in the same degree of "rigorous" (in reality, excessive) detail, as had been the case in the past.

For the reformers, sufficient detail for specified choices was still appropriate, but it was the emphasis on greater scrutiny that was really the strength of our argument. We did not want kids to take things on face value any more. As an example, we might have wanted to say to them that there could be a range of different reasons for that industry being in that place and it may not simply be because the raw materials are relatively accessible. There are likely to be a range of other socio-economic factors at play in this process. This is also likely to be the result of some possibly quite random human decision making. It did not necessarily just happen as it had been traditionally presented. The accusations then came in that these teachers were left-wing because they wanted pupils to ask questions, and in doing so they were challenging the status quo and that they were therefore politicising the classroom for the first time. The perceived logic of that point of view was presumably that discussing things drew attention to shortcomings, awareness of shortcomings led to agitation for change, and, lo and behold, before you knew it you had a revolution on your hands. They needn't have worried, but certainly teachers did operate in different times from today.

The east-west divide was a geopolitical reality and many people felt genuinely threatened by the existence of the Soviet Block, the resulting arms race and perhaps even more so, from the enemy within - socialism. The progressive teachers' response was that the old way of working was itself very political, just political and conservative. It had always implied that you do not question the status quo, just accept it. This is how things are. It is not your job to think about how things can be done better for everyone's benefit. Your job is to learn about it as it is and then feed it back to us after a couple of years, in the way that we want you to.

While those teachers for whom these issues mattered were agonising over all this, not all the activities undertaken in school were too bad. One way of improving how the kids were taught was to get as many classes out of the building doing local field work projects as frequently as possible. The red tape for such ventures was a fraction of what it later became. I really believed in field work. It was active, hands on and experiential. It involved decision making and active co-operation and you could collect and analyse evidence, whether in the form of opinions from interviews, or samples of soil type and vegetation. I hoped that it helped to bring my subject to life.

There were also, I had to admit, some less admirable practices that were still taking place in the 1970s that I took full advantage of. The less able older pupils with relatively short attention spans could often be placated by the overhead projector and the latest piece of South African propaganda about Outspan oranges. I knew quite a bit about politics, as it had been a staple diet of the conversation with my parents throughout my youth. This was a case of needs must, however. I sometimes really required the soporific effect that the blatantly self-serving, pro-government films had on my potentially troublesome youths.

Anything political from either end of the spectrum was supposedly unacceptable territory for teachers to discuss with pupils at that time, though nobody ever objected to the hiring of these films. Indeed, when presented with the opportunity to do so, I always asked for films that were much more closely aligned to the curriculum we were following and nothing to do with the Republic of South Africa, but I was repeatedly told that these more suitable options were not available and so I ended up with what I knew was largely rubbish. We were showered with films of supposedly happy workers in the fields and down the mines. They were provided on hire through the post and without any cost to the school. They swamped whatever alternatives about life in our own country that there might have been around at the time, to such an extent that they were just about the only ones that I could remember making use of, early on. I unashamedly used them as crowd control. I did wonder, however, who had set up this link in the first place. Was it the RSA government that had taken the initiative and simply acquired a list of secondary schools and inundated them with drivel? Who had made those decisions and who paid them? With my fellow geography teachers, I used them as respite, regardless. We sometimes held marathon afternoon film sessions to double-up classes, so that the two teachers could take turns to get a cup of tea and get some paperwork done. The extra class perched on the desks at the back of the room. The black-out curtains in the geography room were drawn, and for an hour or so, fifty or more year ten or year eleven youngsters sat with one teacher, just about in silence, and breathed each other's stale breath. They risked being poisoned by what was on the screen, too, come to think of it.

It is hardly possible to imagine such a situation in modern times. I knew that it was not good education. Eventually, the department bought a TV with a large screen. That is to say a small screen by today's standards, together with a Philips video cassette recorder. Now, that was progress. Later on, the BBC and others would make quality films for specific school subjects. Some, like the two programmes on urban change in Glasgow, would go down as absolute masterpieces. I was at risk of wearing out my copy of them through over-exposure, at the next two schools that I would teach at. These programmes asked questions - and provided uncomfortable answers for some - about how urban Britain was being changed. It was unmistakably political and was totally justifiable, I had concluded.

Throughout the nineteen seventies, I worked with text books that I knew were generally dry, boring and academically unsuitable for use throughout the ability range. Today's young people probably do not have a clue as to how lucky they are in terms of the way that technology has facilitated a wider variety of approaches, more interesting resources and relatively appealing activities.

I also presided over lunch arrangements in the dining hall. The dining hall was actually the rear section of the assembly hall in what was known as the lower school, because it catered for the two years of pupils starting at the age of twelve. The cook supervisor saw to it that I was well rewarded for my efforts, but I ate so much each day that it sometimes made me sleepy after dinner, so I eventually stopped doing it and reverted to taking sandwiches again. The kids were seated around parallel tables holding eight youngsters each and I managed about twenty tables at a sitting, often by myself. Nobody ate a mouthful until all the tables had been served from the hatch by two representatives from each table, and even then, not until everyone was silent sufficiently long enough for me to say grace - *"For what we are about to receive, may the Lord make us truly thankful"*. At the end of the meal, nobody left the hall until the table they were sitting at had been cleaned. For years afterwards, I often thought about how extraordinarily regimented this had been and how well it had worked and how as time went on it would have just become an impossibility due to the changes that were to follow in the relationships between the teachers and the taught.

Eventually, I decided that the time had come for me to be a bit more proactive in my own advancement. I was at a crossroads. It was still not any urge to "get on" that spurred me into action. I was much more concerned with acquiring control over what was taught and how it was taught. We had spoken at home many times about the possibility of moving away and trying something new. I had always been quite sure that I did not want to spend the whole of the rest of my life in our home town, without ever experiencing an alternative. Now that I had become properly qualified and had developed my own ideas about the sort of geography that I wanted to teach, the time had come to look for alternatives, where I could be my own boss, as far as my subject was concerned. I told the head that it was my intention to move on. The leaders at the school gave me the necessary encouragement and support for me to be able to gain promotion elsewhere. I perused the vacancies in the Times Educational Supplement, completed the necessary application forms, sent out a raft of letters and waited to see what happened. In reply to my initial barrage, I received six offers of interviews from all over England. The first one on the list, chronologically in terms of interview dates, was at an all-girls comprehensive school in a town in an old coalfield area, an area that I had frequently drawn maps of on my blackboard as being typical of such landscapes. None of them were particularly close to home, but why move just a few miles away, anyway? That would not be much of a change. I thought that I would take them in the order that they turned up and just see what happened. I was a little surprised to be offered the first job that I went for. Was I to take it or hold out for something potentially more appealing? The trouble was that I could not ask if I could defer judgement until I had seen what all the others had to offer. That was not how it worked. I was expected to say yes or no on the day. I said yes, and so, with our young family, we moved away from our home town.

3. Not St Trinian's

I had actually landed in a bit of an educational backwater. It was a small school - an old girls' grammar school which had turned comprehensive just a year or two earlier. There were well-tended lawns, a number of magnificently maintained grass tennis courts, manicured flowerbeds, established stands of mature trees, a quadrangle with a well-stocked fish pond and a wood panelled library with classical themed and much acclaimed William Morris murals. Closing my eyes while snatching a few minutes of solitude at lunch time, whilst sitting out in the sun on the teak garden benches in front of the school during long summer days, and in an area that was out of bounds to the girls, I thought that there was actually something idyllic about it. It felt like I was in a splendidly presented Victorian park. Then I snapped out of it and went inside to meet the miners' daughters again.

The school had a substantial core of middle-aged staff, many of whom had been there for years during its time as a grammar school. They appeared not to know exactly what had hit them. They were frequently dumbstruck or reduced to tears by the behaviour of their pupils. It was quite a regular event. The staff room door would suddenly fly open and one of the mystified and quickly ageing ladies from another era (when the school had possessed a totally different clientele) would enter, exasperated, flushed and tearful. *"Right, that's it. I've had enough. I'm just sick of them. Can you believe it? I've never seen anything like it in my life. They're just like animals. How rude. It's a disgrace. They show no gratitude. It doesn't matter what*

you do with them. It's always the same. They shout out.
They are just so rude!!". Sinking in to one of the faded and
threadbare armchairs scattered round the edge of the room,
they would then wait to be consoled and comforted by their
colleagues, who were, themselves, probably next in the
firing line. Along the corridor, the girls would be laughing
their socks off at having reduced another of the old dears -
as they no doubt saw them - to tears again, and they would
be looking forward with relish to the next encounter. There
was something rather St. Trinian's-like about it all.

From being an established and highly selective
academic school with an excellent reputation in the town, it
had been turned overnight into a neighbourhood
comprehensive serving the poorest part of the inner urban
area. If there was ever a case of a school being turned on its
head then this was it. I knew that I had been brought in as
one of a few younger - yet experienced - comprehensive
school specialists (or so they hoped). It was assumed,
rightly, as it happened - or so I thought - that I would know
how to speak to ordinary working-class kids without
winding them up by being haughty, dismissive or
constantly scolding in tone. The hope was that as we all
eventually got our act together order would prevail again
and the school would then be able to move forward more
purposefully. The local town centre, a walk of just five
minutes away, looked prosperous enough and coal mining
still employed large numbers of young men throughout the
area.

There were some very old-fashioned looking Victorian
terraces on the way into town, their front doors opening
straight onto the street. Much of the housing from this era

that I had been used to seeing at home had been bulldozed long before. Consequently, there were none of the urban wastelands I was familiar with in the city, where great gaps in the landscape had appeared as the terraces had been demolished, nor was there any need for replacement high-rise blocks of flats, either. The various estates had a settled look by comparison.

The solidarity of the miners and their families was noticeable from articles in the local press, and I soon came across more strongly held anti-monarchist views than I had been used to previously. The more clearly defined and subordinate position of women in society was also evident. Attitudes towards the role of women seemed to have slipped back a generation during the time that it had taken us to make the journey to our new home. Education past the age of compulsion was therefore not really seen as relevant for girls, so there was no point in them staying on at school any longer than they had to. The sooner they got married and moved out, having found another man to tell them what to do, the better.

The school lost a number of potential undergraduates in this way, who insisted on leaving at sixteen-years-old, in spite of being eminently suitable candidates to go on to "A" level and beyond. This was highly likely, I thought, to reflect the pressure that they were under at home for them to leave and get a job and sometimes, no doubt, for very good financial reasons - to further support their families.

I found it much easier, starting the second time round, to establish my own discipline. It was not, as it had been a decade or so before, an insistence on good behaviour based on the threat of violence from somebody else. Those days were largely gone. It was an insistence on good behaviour based on a belief that I would have an answer for whatever was thrown at me, though not necessarily literally. I supposed that it was largely reliant on bluff in the end, but if you could persuade those in front of you that you really believed you could handle them, come what may, then discipline would fall into place. It was down to confidence and as a result I enjoyed a feeling of being firmly in control all the time that I was at that school. I also knew that children were perceptive enough to recognise when their teachers were busting a gut on their behalf and they would tend to treat them accordingly. I settled to the task - indeed, I relished it. I worked very hard, starting early and finishing late every school day for years and years, but I also found considerable job satisfaction in doing it. It was very rewarding for me to see the gradual turn around in the department's fortunes, as measured by the annual examination results.

I revelled in the choice that I had as far as the curriculum and the syllabus were concerned. I chose what I believed were the more progressive interpretations of the subject at "O" level and the Certificate of Secondary Education, choosing there what were known as mode three options, which gave me more latitude again over what was taught and how it would be delivered. I joined a self-help group of like-minded, ambitious and hard-working colleagues in nearby schools within the county, and we collectively developed the new courses, increased the proportion of assessed course work that we could offer and changed our "A" level provision to reflect the latest thinking in the subject, through what was known as the

Schools Council's Project. We arranged field work visits that we could run together and wrote and exchanged various set tasks - meaning challenging learning activities that the kids could get their teeth into, which tested a range of skills and not just factual recall. Our group met regularly to discuss progress and to decide on new ventures. We periodically evaluated the changes that we had made and generally offered each other mutual support throughout each cycle. I believe that it was a gratifying and stimulating experience for all of us. I got to see my colleagues at work, first hand, especially during joint "A" level field courses, and I witnessed some of the best teaching I had ever seen.

I considered that I had established myself as a sound classroom teacher, head of department and form tutor in my new setting. I applied many of the lessons that I had learnt at my first school. The basic tenets of my approach remained simple. Be firm, but show interest. Show them that you have a sense of humour. It is obvious to children if you don't care about them. They will hate your lack of interest more than anything else about you.

The new courses were bedded in and the pupils generally responded appropriately and thrived. I expanded the department effectively, by offering an integrated humanities course for less academic pupils, which was based on 100% coursework. Gradually, exam results improved and the department became recognised as one of the stronger areas within the school. In some years, the results were outstanding across the ability levels within the department, showing what could be done when the will was there and sound judgements were being made about how to use the examination system thoughtfully to cater for the pupils' needs in the most appropriate ways.

I was promoted again. It was not quite so much of a sinecure this time as the position of year head for assemblies had been in my first school, though the pattern was essentially the same. Knowing that we had a young family and only one wage coming in, I thought that the head wanted to be able to thank me, monetarily, for my efforts. The only scale post at her disposal that would allow her to do that was for the running of the Duke of Edinburgh's Award Scheme, usually referred to as the D. of E. I accepted responsibility for that as well and went on to run it at bronze and silver levels for the next eight years.

After a few years, I felt that, overall, I had justified my appointment and repaid the faith which others had placed in me professionally. I had found that the people who were in positions of authority and therefore held critical sway over my fortunes were generally very kind to me throughout the first twenty-three years of my career covering all the time at my first two schools. My first head teacher must have written me a flattering reference, I decided, to elicit a batch of six opportunities to visit schools all over the country for that series of consecutive interviews. The head at my first school had told me afterwards that he had followed up my call to interview with a personal phone call to the lady who was to become my new headmistress. The deputy head at the same school had told me before I left that he had never known anyone who was so popular with both pupils and staff. He was probably trying to instil a bit more self-belief into me prior to interview. I could come over as being a little diffident in my manner, and the last thing that the school wanted from a new appointee was someone who lacked the confidence to make a difference in a new setting. I took some pleasure that my former deputy head had bothered to pay me a compliment at all. Years afterwards, the deputy head at my second school told me that both the head, and she, herself, thought that I was the best appointment that they had ever made.

It is obviously extremely gratifying when senior colleagues choose to share such observations of their own volition, not in answer to a question or because one has tried to put them on the spot. In each case, the observation was spontaneously volunteered and was priceless to me for that one aspect alone. I did not usually go in for self-congratulation or fish for compliments. I didn't even take comfortably or particularly graciously to being praised out loud, feeling instantly self-conscious. I promised myself that I would only mention such things to my wife and nobody else, but I did later rely on reassurances like those because of what was to follow. It would otherwise have been sufficient for me to keep praise received in this way to myself. I believed, rightly, I think, that I had always had the respect and support of my managers throughout this period. Both my head teachers had found a way to reward my efforts, at a time that the scale posts that marked conventional promotion were at a premium. I would take strength from what managers had said to me in previous years, when situations changed.

The local education authority eventually reached the conclusion that the two, separate single-sex schools in the borough, of which ours was one, were too small to continue to operate viably in that fashion, but that a common future would be assured if they were to amalgamate. The opportunity to retain some parental choice within the county for the single sex school option was overlooked in favour of the financial advantages of combining the two institutions. A brief campaign to retain the choice of just one remaining single sex school - as against totally co-educational provision in the town - was virtually over before it had begun. The local authority's insistence on denying parents that simple choice seemed to me to be fundamentally undemocratic. Though I personally would have favoured co-education for myself and our family, not all parents, by any means, shared that view. The obvious choice to continue to offer a degree of diversity was lost.

The staff were all to be transferred over to the new joint school. The newly appointed head teacher and her managers had decided on a faculty system this time. The humanities faculty head would have jurisdiction over geography, history and religious education and would be responsible for leading a team of eleven teachers. I applied for the post and was successful, having been interviewed against four other internal candidates, including three other serving departmental heads. This could have caused a problem straight away. The disappointment the others must have felt at being overlooked could have easily turned into resentment and a degree of negativity, as they would now have to work directly for the person who had just beaten them to the post. It was to their credit as professionals that I was never troubled by such difficulties, for which I was subsequently very grateful. It was effectively my fifth promotion since I had started teaching - year head, officially second in the geography department (no more money, though a little more prestige), head of department, in charge of the D. of E. scheme and now faculty head. Nevertheless, I knew that the challenge ahead would be massive for all sorts of reasons.

4. Just a Bog-Standard Comprehensive?

Whilst still operating as part of an unofficial consortium with other geography teachers in the area, I tried to transfer the best practice from the single-sex school to the new institution. I had to persuade some more traditional teachers, who were now to be part of my expanded geography department, to dispense with some very outdated courses. However, such was the gulf in the respective results from the two departments over the years leading up to the switch that they did not really have a leg to stand on, so I got my own way without much of a fight. The evidence for this approach was incontrovertibly there in black and white for all to see and I also had the backing of the county inspectorate for the changes that I wanted to make.

I retained my enthusiasm for the task ahead and put new practices in place. I enjoyed a generally good rapport with my new colleagues, though it soon became clear which ones were less than enamoured with my presence, by their reluctance to find time to come to some faculty meetings. I would have liked to think that I was an efficient and respected leader of my faculty, but I had to conclude with hindsight that that was probably not a universally held view. Some people who could have made more of an active contribution kept their distance from me and I interpreted that as a mild snub. I had to admit that I had found it easier to galvanise a smaller team as a departmental head, when compared to my new task of coaxing former departmental heads, who had been used to being their own bosses for years, towards a common purpose. It was not easy to inculcate a feeling of togetherness under those conditions. They were all polite and non-confrontational to me on a personal level, though sometimes a little cool and unenthusiastic, especially when I wanted their support for an initiative. I tried to be responsive to their concerns and advocate appropriately on behalf of members of my team, when required, but I was probably not forceful enough on occasions, certainly not sufficiently to impress experienced staff from the former boys' school.

Much of my time in this role was taken up with offering support to, and then dealing with the issues surrounding, the single weak teacher in my faculty. I had actually worked with very few teachers who were blatantly not equipped to do the job they had mistakenly chosen as their career, but this person was one such. In the end, if you gave the impression that you really didn't like children very much you were on a sticky wicket from the start. For such individuals coming to work must have been a daily nightmare. I could not conceive of ever putting myself in that situation in the first place. I hoped that if I had been poor from the start then someone would have taken me aside and told me and I would have gladly gone off and done something else. In teaching, it did not always work like that. A handful of inept operators just carried on against all the odds, day after miserable day. Head teachers always had the power to deal with them, though were sometimes reluctant to use it, perhaps fearing trouble from that teacher's union or a legal challenge, or both. Maybe they just wanted to avoid uncomfortable personal confrontations. The local authority had inspectors to help under such circumstances but they, too, often seemed unable or unwilling to take the bull by the horns.

I had been through this scenario before. A county inspector had tried to make me the mainstay of the case for the prosecution in a campaign to move a colleague out against her will in my previous school. Before he had appeared on the scene, the head herself had already tried to implicate me. I had replied to her that I would continue with my expected monitoring and supportive role towards my struggling colleague, but that I was unwilling to be made the spearhead of the attack on her, other than reporting back to her on any agreed support process.

At this point, I was summoned to a (very) face-to-face meeting with the advisor, as he preferred to be known, in a very small room at the top of the stairs. I was then informed in no uncertain terms that if they wanted to make me the pivotal force in the case against somebody in my department then that was how it was going to be. I would be failing in my duty, he went on, if I were to refuse to follow their instructions.

I simply carried on doing exactly what I had been doing previously and no more than that and the matter was quietly dropped. Nobody ever mentioned it to me again. I considered that both the head and the inspector were just passing the buck, and eventually they just dropped the case and waited until they could persuade this person to take early retirement. In the end, I thought that both of them saw this as the least attractive part of their own jobs and they shied away from it. In short, they copped out.

Suddenly being obliged to get heavy with someone you have worked closely with for some time was not an easy thing to do for a head of department, who rubbed shoulders with that person, day in day out. It was potentially easier for senior staff and the inspectorate to deal with the situation because they did not have that same immediacy in their relationships with their struggling colleague. Consequently, though I had some sympathy with them over it, on the other hand I had never tried to be a head, or indeed to leave the classroom to sit in an office. I had not been in a position to hire someone who was incompetent. It was their cock-up and they could sort it out. I considered that it was their role to make such decisions and not mine. They had certainly chosen not to bite the bullet in this instance, which I imagined was about par for the course, so poor teachers were occasionally allowed to struggle on to absolutely no-one's advantage. Even when they were moved on, they could end up at another school. I was told that one even came back again to the school that had finally managed to get rid of them after years of trying. I had no idea how that could have happened but apparently it did. Maybe the teacher concerned threatened to bring a case for wrongful dismissal and they didn't fancy a public battle. Perhaps it was just supply and demand again and they could not fill a vacancy with anyone else at short notice, so it could have been a case of better the devil you know than a string of variable supply teachers who you don't know. To put this affair into context, most teachers I had met had done a very good job. These poor souls that become problems for everyone for years and years were very few and far between. You go into teaching because you want to help kids. People do it in different ways and, of course, some are better at it than others.

I had by now settled into my third long stretch at a different comprehensive school. As my third decade progressed, however, I developed a gradual feeling of unease which grew to serious disquiet and then finally to really disturb my attitude to the job that I had hitherto loved doing. It was largely about the internal politics of the school, though, in reality, it was actually impossible to separate those issues from the changes that were taking place in the immediate community that we served and in society at large.

Exasperation led to frustration at my inability to affect change for the better. I reached the point where I felt that I had to start to write down what was happening just to enable me to get my head around it on a daily basis and in time for me to face the next instalment. I needed to find a way to respond to circumstances that were clearly going to carry on mounting up. In so doing, I was only too aware that I was taking important preparation time away from my pupils and redirecting it to comparatively self-indulgent concerns. I just felt that I had to do it to survive.

I started my diary in September 1994, one year into the new co-educational school, and kept it going until the end of my teaching career in schools, in the summer of 2005. Though now rewritten and adapted for this purpose, it still contains the essentials of the issues I faced, sufficient to communicate the flow of events. In its original hand-written form, it was over two hundred pages of A4 plus various newspaper extracts.

5. Staying Afloat

This was the first time I had tried to make sense of any of my previous educational experiences and to record them in a meaningful way. I had by then at least gained some degree of perspective afforded by the passage of time. Looking back, it surprised me that the problems that beset us had started to arise so early on in the life of the new joint school.

What was different by the summer of 1994 and only one year into the coeducational setting, was that I had started to feel bitter about aspects of the situation I found myself in. My career spanned the birth and development of comprehensive schooling. I have always been in favour of it. This emanated from the dissatisfaction I felt with my own grammar schooling and the divisiveness I was aware of, even within that building. My parents faced a dilemma in the Sixties. As middle-class socialists with their values and attitudes firmly founded in benevolent, non-conformist Christian beliefs, they did not need to have the flaws of the selective system explained to them. They had benefited from it themselves, of course, and Dad, particularly, had a long-standing devotion to his old school, the same one that I had passed the eleven plus exam for and which he had previously attended as a scholarship boy. Yet, when the time for change came, he was more concerned with choosing the right name for the place than the actual fact of its going comprehensive. I had objected to so much that went on in the grammar school, including the obsession with uniformity, the aping of the public schools, the pontificating delivered from the platform, the supposed superiority they tried to imbue in us, the remote formality of addressing boys by their surnames and the straight-jacket of the streaming system.

Working in a large, mixed comprehensive school was, on paper, therefore, an opportunity for me to put my ideals into practice. From the off, however, the daily issues we faced were necessarily much more parochial. Ever since the early days of the new school and as new systems bedded in, I had concerns about the nature of the workload being placed on the four faculty heads and in particular about the extent of our pastoral responsibilities. I discussed this - at least in part - with the head, the deputy head and our local education authority's secondary phase inspector. The core of the problem was the proportion of time demanded by pastoral matters and the draining effect this had by the end of the day on my ability to plan positively for the future. I knew that long term improvements in results depended on my finding the time and energy to devise appropriate teaching strategies and classroom activities.

Throughout the first year of the new school, I had found it just about impossible to meet all the demands being placed on me, at the same time as having a pretty full timetable and a form teacher's role. Withdrawal room duty (a kind of manned sin bin, open all day, every day, to accommodate naughty children who would not behave in lessons), manning detentions and being nominal first port of call for all the miscreants in my faculty, with all the attendant paperwork and counselling requirements, seemed like a considerable overload from the off.

In the past, there had been a much more clearly defined dichotomy between pastoral and curricular responsibilities, which had worked well in my experience. Now this distinction had been purposely blurred. I felt frustrated that as the whole school policy unfolded and new structures were put into place and even abridged, the central concerns of the small group of faculty heads were being overlooked. I didn't see how I could find the opportunities to develop the curricular side of things whilst I had so much of everything else to do, yet it was the curricular side of the job that especially appealed to me.

I understood the theory behind the new set up. It was based on the premise that children misbehave primarily when the teaching stimulus is inappropriate. There was obviously some truth in this and I recognised my responsibility to provide appropriate tasks within the faculty. That was not, however, the whole story, or even the central issue. We had a significant number of pupils who brought their behavioural problems to lessons across the board, regardless of what they were being offered.

Nevertheless, the implication was being made straight away in our new school that it was the teachers' fault that there was bad behaviour in lessons. Since Rosla, in my first year of teaching, I had involved myself in choosing whatever new syllabuses were available that seemed to offer an improvement compared to what had gone before. Each involved enormous time invested in new classroom activities and strategies. For some children, I had never found a solution that had quite worked. Plus, it seemed iniquitous to me that the best way to deal with a conflict situation in the classroom was to jettison the pupil to a colleague who already had a class, as was to happen again that year in the lower school, thus disrupting the progress of another thirty pupils unnecessarily and adding to the stress levels of a teacher already under pressure. I didn't believe that it was right that at the same time as this was happening, experienced, successful and more senior teachers, who were theoretically available to be called on for assistance, were now deciding to concern themselves with tasks that had somehow assumed more importance than offering direct help to the classroom teacher. Those who already had the greatest pupil contact time were being told to just pass disruptive children around between themselves rather than involve those who really had the time to deal with them.

I had welcomed the appointment of two new pastoral posts. At last, it seemed that the greater flexibility this offered would release some of the pastoral responsibilities from the faculty heads. My frustration was compounded by the apparent "no change" to the policy. This was especially so, because after the summer of 1994 more senior pastoral staff had acquired even more non-contact time, whilst my contact time and that of some of other faculty heads had actually increased.

In March 1995, the deputy head shared with us a report that she had written for the governors. In it, she suggested that many of the staff believed that discipline in the school was the responsibility of the senior management team alone. This was then described as an abdication of responsibility on the part of the staff concerned. She went on to say that some colleagues were abusing the on-call system, allowing bad behaviour to continue and not recognising it as their problem to sort out, individually. This meant that as far as the management were concerned, the structures our leaders had set up were being purposely by-passed, which had obviously not been their intention, at all.

The feeling from above had been made crystal clear to the governors and to us. We struggled on, but after two years of the situation, by September 1995, I had decided that for the first time in my career I was teaching in a school that was truly awful. This conclusion was immediately confirmed by my worst field trip ever, courtesy of six naughty girls, and then returning to school in the afternoon to hear stories and read referrals about what I'd missed whilst I was in the hills. One teacher had been pushed in the chest by a pupil, another pushed from behind in the dinner queue, a third not only having paper thrown in his face and a cigarette lit in his class, but had also suffered pupils spitting on his clothing.

The faculty heads had been appointed to take charge of the whole teaching curriculum, split into four sections. It was abundantly clear by then that that we were very much the focal point of the pastoral system as well. We had become a choke point within the school's hierarchy. It felt like all problems from below came to us, and they were then effectively ours to deal with. We were also uncertain about what role the local education authority's secondary phase inspector had, and how he might be able to help us, or at least listen to our point of view. He had personally encouraged me to make my views clear to a review team, which presumably the authority had set up on his say so, and maybe at the first indications of disquiet, either from us or from elsewhere. He insisted to me that it was a two-way process. He even stopped me on his way out of school one day while I was on drive duty to tell me this again. I was somewhat mystified. He had already told me he didn't believe in "bull shine". I think that is what he said. I had a rough idea of what he meant.

He missed, by a day or two, a mass riot down the road, when a mob from our place went out at lunchtime to hand out some local hospitality to kids from another school, who they somehow found out were doing field work in the town centre.

It was hardly surprising that we were having a problem with the kids. The immediate area had become very depressed, economically. Mining and textiles had completely folded. The town had lost all three of its pits within 10 years. The town's unemployment rate was 16% and our district of the county had the fastest rising unemployment rate in England and Wales between 1981 and 1991. We had the poorest catchment in the town. 13 out of the 24 pupils in my class in that year were on free dinners. Many parents were now long term unemployed and there was increasing evidence in school of the breakdown of the traditional family unit. Aspiration often appeared to be dismally low and still falling. When I had asked a lad in my class a question at parents' evening and he was a little slow to answer, his mum kicked him under the table to exact a response. I found that quite disturbing but somehow indicative of a much wider unhappiness.

I had a good moan to myself about the "management from a distance" idea that now prevailed. I saw it as Ofsted-speak and Thatcherism in practice, finally having sifted its way down to the schools, where I considered that it was a fundamentally flawed idea. As I saw it, the aim was to make schools into businesses by making them compete against others until the comparatively unsuccessful ones went to the wall and the winners took the spoils, except, of course, that schools were not businesses. They did not sell a product. They dealt with people and hopefully prepared them all for a full life in society. If this remote management style was to be part of it, why bother appointing teachers to manage us, at all? Why not get managers from industry and commerce? It had given the head and the first deputy head exactly the justification they sought for the changes that they had made.

Managers in schools had previously seen their prime responsibility as servants of the classroom teacher from the moment that they were newly appointed. They saw that as their duty and they believed it was the best way of helping the pupils in the classroom, and they were right. Managers in schools were still teachers, who had presumably been promoted because they were good at it, with some notable and perceptible extra leadership qualities to offer at a higher level.

By November 1995, it became clear that we were being faced with a further 10% cut in resources again for the next year (four teachers' worth). As a departmental manager of my subject, I was getting less to spend each year, yet inflation and the cost of resources carried on rising relentlessly. The decision to squeeze the public sector financially, alongside a drive for greater efficiency via the adoption of industrial style management, had only hit us in that last couple of years, it seemed, and therefore it had coincided with the setting up of our new school. It looked to me as though budget cuts were to be the cost to us of income tax reductions planned to buy another term in office, so that those who had kept a job benefited twice over those who had recently lost theirs.

I had some more immediate concerns, as well. Friday was a bad day, I wrote. I met the mother of a boy in my class at 8.10 a.m., another haggard, battle-weary woman. She was aghast (on the face of it, at least) at the litany of her son's misdemeanours and in particular at his swearing at staff. The lad had intercepted the post on the day my letter arrived at home inviting her to school. The previous time I had occasion to write home to a parent, the boy's mother told me at parents evening, *"My husband is the only one allowed to get the post in our house. My son knows that"*. In this case, Mum was rightly disappointed in her son's attitude, but how much of his behaviour was a response to the regime at home? *"If the police had seen him when I'd sorted him out on Tuesday, I'd have been in trouble"*, she said. *"Wait till his dad gets in. We've tried everything with him. He's not coming to school today"*. She meant it. She asked me to send him to her at 8.40 when he arrived. I did. He didn't go. I took him to her and she took him home. I told her that his response to my request for him to go to meet her had been, *"Oh fucking hell"*. In retrospect, I was amazed that I had stuck the boot in like that. She bundled him out of the main door, the scuffle attracting not just my attention but that of others who were passing. I thought, Oh my God, I've set him up for such a beating.

I told the head that I was worried about what lay in store for him. She requested me to ask the second deputy head to ring social services to let them know that we were concerned about his fate. He asked the secretary to do it. The head saw me later and asked me if I had followed it up, because we had to cover ourselves in such situations.

What about the boy? Occasional nuisance that he was, I felt sorry for him. I don't know what he received over the weekend that followed, but I knew that it wouldn't have cured him. I bet that was why he was like that in the first place. *"It didn't do me any harm"*, his mother had added. Yes, it did, I thought. It actually did irreparable damage to you, so much so that you pass the damage on through the next violent generation to the one after that. I wanted no further part in it. It stank. I decided that I'd let him swear rather than send him home again to get beaten up if that was the case - assuming that he was to re-surface. I comforted myself with the notion that if he was to abuse me, I was, by tolerant reasoning, showing him a better way to behave. Perhaps that was the only way to break the cycle. Our influence seemed to be so limited and peripheral at times like that. We saw so little of these kids individually. They didn't want to talk to us much, anyway. I wondered if we sometimes tended to over-estimate the influence that we had to affect things for the better. We actually needed to employ a full-time, fully trained social worker and a child psychiatrist to allow some of our children to fully benefit from being there.

On the last day of the month, I broke up a fight. It was a very public affair. A throng of about 200 were baying for blood in a public place, just at the end of the main drive. So much violence, which was unfortunately only too typical of the way they sometimes related to each other. Self-esteem was at the root of this. The pecking order thing all came down to self-esteem. If you were happy with yourself and where you were at, you didn't need to go around doing all that strutting your stuff posing and posturing, then feeling obliged to back it up, if it was questioned, with a bit of unrestrained aggression. The trouble was that their low self-esteem impacted on ours. Teachers increasingly gained a sense of a lack of self-worth because they felt helpless in the face of fairly major problems day after day. They didn't believe that they were performing adequately. They actually hoped everyone else had the same problems as they did. They took comfort, perversely, from tales of trouble elsewhere in the building, but the feeling that I was not coping as I wanted to consistently gnawed at me. I felt that my response to being left to my own devices and closing down any reliance on other people from outside the room was likely to be to cut corners, lower my own standards, and appease more in the long run, just to get by.

I knew that the standard of work would be the first casualty if that happened. *The kids are all right if you let them get on with their chat",* I'd heard more than once, except, unfortunately, that their chat often got nasty and deteriorated alarmingly into a downward spiral that led to an intensely stressful atmosphere. It could quickly degenerate from argument to physical attacks that could then risk spilling out of the room into more public areas. As a priority, you wanted to keep your troubles in your own room, otherwise you were advertising your problems to the world.

My reward for stopping the recent fight was a chat with a naughty boy's stepfather. The head of science had managed to *"coax"* the boy out of the science block. The boy decided that this was assault and his dad was *"coming up to school to sort it out"*. It was to be the form tutor in his pastoral role who would be in the firing line and that was me.

At the start of the new term in January 1996, the new science teacher lasted 3 days and 2 lessons. He walked out and was followed by a supply teacher who dipped her toes in for less than a day. We (the four heads of faculties) all had a good moan to our secondary phase inspector after school and at his invitation. He said we should write down what is wrong, behaviour-wise, and say what should be done about it. We said this was déjà vu for us. We had made our observations and recommendations during the previous year and they had been ignored. He set up the head to meet the middle managers the next day. The meeting was a bit of a damp squib. The inspector concentrated on behaviour, identifying bullying and lack of respect as areas to focus on. The head sat impassively, making no comment, even when it was pointed out that staff felt it was them that were being monitored by their use of the on-call system, rather than the pupils.

An incident occurred involving the second deputy head and a colleague in my department. I took the results of the monitoring of her class's behaviour to the second deputy after briefing. He told me he would see it through with letters home etc, but that I should discount certain references from my colleague on the grounds that it had been her fault rather than theirs and that she had behaved unreasonably. It put me in a difficult position. By chance, I met my colleague more or less immediately afterwards and decided to tell her the situation. I felt the second deputy had been unreasonable towards me and to her. I felt she needed my support as a member of my team, and that was more important than keeping a confidence with the second deputy, which was based, in my judgement, on a less than satisfactory observation by him of her role in the matter. The second deputy then joined us and my colleague put her concerns to him directly. I suggested we should be discussing it somewhere more private and so we went to the meeting room and talked it through. I said that although I had possibly breeched his confidence, he had put me in a very difficult position and that my first loyalty was to my colleague. The second deputy said he accepted this. He spoke to me again, privately, afterwards. He said he was disappointed that I had felt it necessary to tell my colleague what he had said to me. I said I thought I had made the right judgement. He said he hoped that we were now working together as one staff and that this would be our main chance of impressing Ofsted. I said that I had told the head that if I thought that things were wrong then I would tell her directly, as I had before, or I would raise matters in the appropriate forums for such discussions.

In early February 1996, I heard that at least two other departments had run out of money, as well. I was also told that one (thus far un-named) member of staff had spent an incredible amount going on courses in the same academic year. I guessed that this was unlikely to be a chalk face worker and according to a cleaner, the same person had also spent £8,000 on office furniture, but not for the main part of the school. Meanwhile, I re-used envelope files and card file dividers. I picked up any pens left lying around in my room to replace those pinched from me and I stole paper clips from wherever I happen to be sitting, around the place.

Whilst supposedly enjoying the benefits of a "free" period, as we optimistically called them, I was summoned to assist my special needs colleague. I had never heard so much screaming and yelling - he was with my tutor group as well. Then it was straight to another faculty colleague with a bit of bother. That member of staff was quite rude to me when I went to help, really uptight and not even fully coherent by the time I got to the room. I offered to take three of the class into my room, which was by chance empty at the time. They did some quiet colouring in, while one of them told the others about a girl he claimed to have had in his bed at the county's field study centre, bringing a whole new meaning to off-site extra-curricular activities.

The union conference was more interesting than it had been in most years, attention being focussed on bad behaviour, and somewhat belatedly, on the responsibilities that parents had in that regard. Meanwhile, a former member of my faculty had reportedly won a case at a tribunal for unfair dismissal from our school. The understanding was that the settlement included a clause preventing them from going to the press.

Union representatives let it be known that a sudden, perplexing but noticeable amelioration in management attitude at the beginning of the previous term had its origin in officers of the union having put pressure on senior members of the county inspectorate, who in turn put pressure on the head to change course, which she then seemed to have done. Meanwhile, I had helped to split up 3 fights during that term, which was a record for me.

Ofsted came in May. I sat and listened to the department's feedback in the deputy head's office. On the way downstairs afterwards, the Ofsted inspector cut out the jargon and said, "*I think geography will emerge as one of the stronger areas of the school*". I heard that English, maths and history did OK, too. I wondered who was going to cop it. We couldn't have been that good, especially as the head had dropped her new approach that very morning in briefing, berating us for not challenging bad behaviour in the classroom, which had apparently led to low marks in some areas of the feedback.

I had scored one 4 (on of a 1 to 7 scale), which was satisfactory, and the rest were 3s (good). Nearly lost in all the Ofsted excitement was the case of the school in the city where the staff had refused to teach a naughty boy and got national media attention for days afterwards. They won, but more importantly it showed clearly how far the pendulum had swung by then in favour of dysfunctional families. His mother had also apparently assaulted someone. It highlighted just what we had to face and gave national prominence to the problem of disruption.

We had passed. The judgement was that the senior management team was strong and that the problems were caused by weak teachers. It felt to me like a complete travesty and a total misrepresentation of what had happened over the previous three years. We thought it must have been the management that was going to cop it, but not so. I just couldn't believe that they hadn't seen through them. It was a re-run of the deputy head's original letter to the governors. We were gob-smacked. We had been stitched up. Where on earth, could we go from there?

What it seemed to amount to was that corporate-style management really had arrived. Supporting teachers in the classroom was no longer their function. They were there to manage firmly and that is what they would do. They had their systems in place and we had to do what they said. If we couldn't do it, it would be our fault not theirs. If people really thought that schools were like factories the future was gruesome. I felt like I was in the wrong place on that day. I had never felt that I did not belong in school before.

True to form, the local paper chose to run a doom and gloom headline for our Ofsted report, anyway, and the head was reported to have been "very angry". I heard it on good authority that there was already a knock-on effect in terms of middle school pupils who would normally have come to us choosing to go elsewhere, in addition to the annual haemorrhaging of more capable children with more discerning parents, that we habitually incurred to the benefit of our two nearest comprehensives. There were real fears for our long-term future. Although the immediate pressure was temporarily off, with the exam years having left and Ofsted behind us, the atmosphere actually became incredibly relaxed, or, more accurately, totally disinterested. Nobody wanted to debate anything, and everything went through on the senior management team's say so.

At the end of the summer term, I met one of the physical education staff at a concert. He told me (very hush, hush and via the union) that HMI would be in school during the next year and that they would be directing their visit at the senior management team.

By the autumn term of 1996, the first deputy was officially in charge of the curriculum, so it was to her that I went for the geography exams feedback meeting. I said I did not get enough money to run the department properly. She said she was sympathetic and would try to press the governors to pay less on structure and more on curriculum. It sounded like platitudes. We would see if she was successful, but I doubted it.

The base of the first deputy's new empire was the school office. I called it Fortress Bureaucracy. It happened gradually, by stealth - restricted opening hours, early closing, blinds erected, notices posted and the withdrawal of services previously offered. To gain attention, we then had to ring the bell, queue with the kids, while they (the office staff and members of the senior management team), were standing or sitting around gabbing on the inside, while we were marooned there on the outside, feeling like prats and second-class prats, at that. At the staff meeting, I questioned whether the office really needed to be closed at lunch time at all.

We were informed that the Queen was coming to visit us on the 21st March. She would officially open the new bits of the school. To mark the occasion, £100,000 was to be spent on an Elizabethan style garden right outside my classroom window. On my side of the wall, separating me from the garden, the ill-fitting window frames, one held in place with a rusty nail, would continue to let the draught in, whilst the surrounding plaster work would carry on crumbling. What strange contradictions there are in this business, I thought. Suddenly, literally millions were to be spent on buildings, with more to come, apparently, including a revamped pavilion, whilst simultaneously, staff were fewer, day-to-day resources harder to come by, administrative tasks increasing and management by action point having replaced the human touch.

I was never much of a monarchist. I knew the pros and cons, but it all seemed a bit anachronistic and undemocratic in a supposedly modern meritocracy. More immediately, it brought out the grovelling, creeping sycophants and hangers-on and showed them at their worst. They were around soon enough, striding the path that the Queen would take, planning and posing, discussing and scheming and no doubt jostling for position - the closer the better. I hated this deferential, know your place nonsense. What about the kids? It was not a shopping centre or a factory. Would they get a look in if they wanted one and how would they be selected? On the other side of the walls, the disaffected and disadvantaged youth of the town would continue to be ignored and marginalised from the mainstream in their own community and society at large, while grasping outsiders would elbow their way in and be wooed by the chairman of the governors, in return for some future favour or influence that we will never hear about. Then, HM would be gone and school would just carry on as before, bathing in gradually diminishing reflected glory, as harsh reality seeped back in day by day.

I got caught out one day by not thinking on my feet the day before. The first deputy warned us in briefing that the senior management team would be formally monitoring the application of the school's action plan. The second deputy then pounced, asking me for the two impositions I should have given to two boys who were late to school. I said, admittedly in a rather contrite fashion, that I had overlooked it. I then had to set about putting things right, causing a confrontation with the two boys concerned, who were unlikely to meet the Queen under any circumstances and who were not expecting a punishment at all, never mind one issued a day late. I asked the second deputy for his assistance to see it through. There is no way that I was going to sit down with that boy's aggressive mother again and tell her that "this is his last chance". I insisted that the second deputy did it (though, admittedly, he did not know it at that point in time).

In February 1997, a whole stream of well-argued and pertinent points, primarily about the ridiculous daily office closures, pushed the first deputy further and further into a corner at the staff meeting, until she snapped and made a personal comment about one of the young science teachers. What typified the debate was not just the list of apposite points being made, but who was making them. Not the jaded, weary faculty heads (now ex-faculty heads, of which more later), who had slunk off with their tails between their legs in abject defeat months beforehand, but the new wave of younger colleagues, the more recent appointees of the management over the previous few years.

I knew that schools were not democracies. Yet schools are part of the liberal democratic tradition in this country, in which issues are open to debate amongst colleagues of different rank, even if in the end the veto comes down and we have to comply with the wishes of those that get justly rewarded for the responsibility of making the final decision. I was OK with that. We would have had our say, got things off our chests, aired our grievances, tried to get some empathy going for our point of view, felt we had been listened to, even if it appeared that our senior colleagues had forgotten some pretty harsh realities, once promotion had come their way. It appeared, however, that criticism was increasingly being interpreted as a personal attack and not issue-based. A fear of spontaneity had emerged. I sensed a lack of confidence amongst the management in facing democratic discussion. Escape clause clichés were trotted out, more and more, such as, *"It is noted", "your comments have been taken on board", "we will come back to you on that one", "leave it with me",* or *"this is not the right forum for this topic of discussion".*

Next, I was in trouble with the official monitoring of the action plan once again. Everyone in my class had failed the uniform check. I submitted my list of colourful miscreants and nothing happened, to me or to them. There followed a "no coats on in the classroom" check from the management, working in pairs like late-night inner-city policemen. Why didn't I get a visit? After all, I failed the uniform test badly. I was almost beginning to feel left out. My pre-prepared little speech, if they were to take me to task over uniform, ran to the effect that I got the best "A" level results in school last year and the best GCSE results the year before, because I wasn't wasting good learning time picking arguments with them over their wish for some reasonable level of self-expression over clothing choices.

I noted that the head seemed to be getting tough with some individual teachers; tough with the deputy head of science for not applying the code of conduct over uniform and tough with a seasoned English teacher for not having a positive attitude, though he had been there for decades, was a steady performer with good discipline and was popular with the kids. Tough, also, with a technology teacher, who was told that it was his responsibility when kids from his class messed about in somebody else's physical education class.

Then, it felt like the head was getting tough with me, too, or rather not directly with me but with a pleasant, hard-working and quite bright girl, whose crime was that her folks had arranged a family holiday that clashed with a geography field visit. I asked the head if I could move the date of the trip to accommodate the girl and she came back to me and said she was making a stand. The senior management team had discussed it and there had been far too much of it. Attendance was important, she added, and too many parents had been taking their kids out of school and we really needed to get tough with them. She was going to talk to the girl and her parents, if necessary. I told the head that the girl was in good faith and just got caught in the middle. I just wanted to be as flexible as I could and offer her the same chance as the others. I had checked the calendar and saw no obvious clashes. Bewilderingly, the head asked me why parents do it. I told her that holidays were half the price in term time that they were during school holidays, so a pretty good reason if you were strapped for cash. I was tempted to tell her that there were 100 kids in school that she could take a firm line with, but that she had chosen not to, because she would get too much flak from them and in some cases from their parents, too. Instead, she had wanted to risk alienating a perfectly good kid, with kind and supportive parents over nothing at all.

By March, the Queen's visit was imminent and what a performance it was. The Elizabethan garden was completed, walls were painted, paths cleaned, school gates restored, stone work pressure hosed, sculpture erected, toilets re-tiled, wooden floors polished, carpets laid, plaque put in place, new flag poles pointed to the sky, turfs laid, seating set out, displays arranged, honours boards updated, bins removed (?), public address system set up, security cameras attached and whirring, monitors scrutinised, thousands of invitations issued and key personnel primed about how to "bob" and not "curtsey".

Republicans were moaning, royalists were creeping and opportunists were asking if they could stay inside and take the photographs and being told they could. It could have been raining. I would not have to stand out in the cold with my pleurisy-weakened right lung muscles. I could opt out of cheering and flag waving legitimately and would still be able to contribute to the school's efforts, by hopefully recording the event appropriately. I was told it would be just me that would receive this special dispensation and that I couldn't use flash photography. I was just about comfortable with all this, though some fervent anti-royalists had already scowled their disapproval in my direction, even though one of them drove a mini with a union jack painted onto its roof. Perhaps that was to throw people off the republican scent.

The head capitulated over the field work issue, perhaps because she was dealing with a demonstrably nice girl, or perhaps because the she was too busy preening herself for the big day to be bothered any more. What a fuss over nothing - the girl, I meant, though thinking on, definitely both.

In the spring I always got worried about the course work files because of the internal moderation process. I was in sole charge of this and I never got it quite right to my own satisfaction. I sent the sample to the exam board thinking either that I had been more than fair to my colleagues and less than fair to my own kids or I had been fair to my kids, but felt uncomfortable about whether my colleagues were completely happy with my decisions, even if they didn't say so. Every year I expected to be challenged by the moderator for messing it up. In my 15 years as a head of department up to that moment, I never had been. Nevertheless, I was so worried this time, that I had already written the initial notes for my defence in the front of my planner, so I could tell him straight away when he rang up to complain. This is why, in a nutshell, I could never have been relaxed in an atmosphere demanding high-powered decision making. In essence, it is why I had peaked where I was then. I admitted it. I was not comfortable with decision making that judged the professional competency of other colleagues. I would have made a rubbish manager at a higher level. I would have tied myself in knots by being able to see both points of view at every turn and in doing so, I would have regularly fallen into the enormous chasm that was just gaping there and waiting for me between any two stools.

The Queen came and went in forty minutes. With no flash on the camera and at a considerable distance from all the action on the stage, I had to admit that I did not capture Her Majesty for posterity quite as well as I might have done, had I been a little less overawed by the combination of the importance to the school of the occasion and my own added responsibility. Keeping a very modestly priced zoom lens steady, and clicking the button as slowly as I could so as not to make any unnecessary noise and at such a slow speed in poor indoor light, whilst perched on the balcony right at the back of the hall, would have tested the best, surely, not just a perspiring teacher with unusually shaky hands? Yet, to my knowledge, in a cupboard in my office lay one of the only two sets of pictures in the public domain (HM also had her own photographic record keeper at these events, it seemed) of a reigning monarch on the premises in the history of our four-hundred-year-old school.

Our next visitors were to be HM's inspectors, though obviously there was no direct connection with the recent appearance of HM. I got my schemes of work up to date and an analysis of our results prepared. I wasn't averse to "rigour", the in-vogue word of the times. Real improvements, however, would come from teachers being motivated, and that was dependent on time, incentives, support and resources. The measuring of performance that the politicians were then now so openly keen on in order to improve their own ratings, was a sideshow, by comparison. The national debate at the time about standards and choice in education was missing the point. It was all peripheral to us. We served this heavily disaffected area, a concentration of poor people in a struggling town. They felt overlooked. They had no real choice. They couldn't get their children into our rival local schools because they were already full and to some extent because some of the kids who might have naturally come to us had already chosen to go there.

Private education was way out of their reach. Parents could not afford the inconvenience of time and money to send their children further afield, even if they wanted to. Many were without access to a car. Many more could not find extra bus fares to send their children any distance from home on a daily basis. Nor could they have afforded to move to a nicer home with a nicer school in a nicer catchment area. So, what was their choice, in all that, then? Where were their children to go to school? It was not even their main concern. Nor was that their fault. It wasn't that they didn't care about their kids, in most cases, either. Schooling was just a bit further down their list of priorities, after having a job, receiving reasonable pay, living in decent housing, having access to nearby shops and services and fitting in the demands of what were often unsociable working hours around the family's varied requirements.

In May 1997, I recorded a wobble, by which I meant I got visibly stressed. It could get to me for the rest of the day and I might then take it out on people at home a bit. My wife obviously recognised it and explained it to anyone else who might have noticed. I managed because I never let it spoil the next day. I had always got over it, thus far, anyway. It tended to happen on rapid fire days, when I moved all day from one event to another. Strangely, I couldn't ever see them coming. They just happened. Then I was in them. Bang, bang, bang - uncomfortable social interactions, one after the other.

This one happened after a morning that went swimmingly well. Then, all of a sudden, I had a rubbish lesson, followed by a difference of opinion with a lad outside my room, leading to him telling me to "*piss off*", a parent to see me straight after school to complain about my allowing his daughter to walk down a busy road alone after a field visit, so that I was then late to the heads of department's meeting. I had no time to eat a snack or find a clean cup for some coffee, and I rounded the day off with a sheaf of targets and ultimatums handed to me by the deputy head that I wasn't expecting, and there I was in a thoroughly bad mood, irreconcilable for the rest of the evening.

In the same month, my class left for study leave, as we euphemistically and optimistically called it. I had to say goodbye to my young "friend", an ever present to the end, who was now reported to be up on a charge for stabbing somebody elsewhere. He was polite to me to the last, however, following the "chat" I had "enjoyed" with his mum. With some regret, I had not returned the reference I had received for his application to join the army, the day before he left. He had been generally OK with me, though I thought that he was probably able to wind up other kids and then appear to be relatively blameless when it came to the crunch. I'm sure he didn't fear me at all, though as his form tutor, he knew that I was the one with the hotline to his mum.

There was always something exciting about a union meeting called at short notice. I went along expecting a revelation but usually didn't get one. This one revolved around lunchtime cover. The school employed people to come in and do it. Now, we had been put down to do it, without any negotiation. As far as we were concerned, lunchtime was sacrosanct and not negotiable. I had also noticed the ease with which management arranged meetings at times when they were down to do their little bit of teaching, meaning that we then had to cover for them.

I got all wound up before half term, ready to talk about the lack of a forum for democratic discussion, but the opportunity never arose, which rather proved my point. I invigilated a business studies exam and one of the questions was, "*What sorts of management are there?*" The boy whose script I had on top of the pile at the end had put quite correctly, I would guess, "*democratic, laissez-faire and autocratic*". He was certainly on the right track, anyway. I knew which one was in favour at our school.

By June, our right to run our own budgets as departmental heads had been taken away from us. The reason given was that the school was skint, so we had to take particular care to stay within spending limits. Our cooperation was sought on the grounds that the senior management team had assured us that there would be no redundancies amongst the teaching staff in that year. It felt to me like I couldn't be trusted to make the sort of decisions I had been making satisfactorily for the previous 15 years and that I was not professional enough to run my area without veto. There was no further discussion about it and so the running of the school became a stage more centralised than it had been before.

Next, we discovered that there were plans afoot to reduce the range of "A" levels that the school offered at a stroke. There was to be no more music, chemistry, religious education, sociology, German, French, or even history - though that department had the second-best results in the school in 1996. We were not told about who wanted to do what, in terms of "A" level pupil preferences, as expressed by the then current potential sixth formers in year eleven.

Hot foot from my one-to-one with the head, I had got out without being asked to do anything extra, so that meant it had gone well. It was a close call, though. She reminded me that I was one of only two people in the school on protected points. The head of faculty roles had been done away with in 1995, supposedly to save money and effectively demoting the four of us, in favour of a return to heads of department, only. The head was implying that I was therefore in a privileged position, with which I had to agree. I said there was no way I could take on any more, but that I was just coping. That was exactly the case.

I had asked the head if the budgetary change was a permanent arrangement and she said she had been put in a difficult position. She had had to ask the governors for an extra £12K to cover the anticipated shortfall resulting from a prematurely announced over-commitment on their part. The governors had apparently stumped up, but by the year's end we actually ended up carrying over £20K. That had been an awkward sequence of events to justify, which was hardly surprising, but one which had clearly been an embarrassment. Perhaps people had done what I did, namely, spent very carefully in 1996-97, because they felt there was not enough to run their departments in 1995-96, when they were conscious that they were running out of cash by February. I had said that after 11 years of no problems at my previous school, I had found it difficult to balance the books in each year of the new school, thus far. I don't know if the head really recognised the pressure everyone was under.

Day to day confrontations were not easing either. I was first on the scene one lunchtime, when a lad kicked a dinner lady. In some places that would have been a major event, but it didn't even make the basis for an informal staff room after dinner discussion. After school on the same day, I was first present again, in the company of one other colleague, to unclog human congestion at the bottom of the drive. You knew straight away what causes those knots of kids. There was a pattern the bodies made facing inwards, visible from any distance, leading to apprehension and general unease, as you approached. For me it was deep breathing and a determination not to cop out. Closer in, it was easy to see where the trouble was, even amongst 100 plus kids. They guided your eyes because they were all looking at the protagonists as well. *"What's going on, then?"* Nobody answered, or even looked at me. It was like I was invisible. At that moment, I could have just been another kid as far as they were concerned. *"Off you go then, go home, you are blocking the drive"*, I said, with as much authority as I could muster. Luckily, on this occasion, there was dispersal. They moved down to a side road, off the premises, but still only 50 yards away from the school gates and fewer of them this time. I did not follow them. Last time, I had. It was horrible. I ended up trying to break through a sealed ring of kids baying and shouting at the two girls who were fighting. This time I left them to it. I did not hear anything about it at all the next day. Everyone had new problems to face. It was just water under the bridge. Another day of failing to deal adequately with everyday challenges.

In June, we learnt that the governors had put the blocks on the senior management team's decision to stop GCSE and "A" level music running on the grounds that group sizes opting for the subject were too small. Apparently, parents had gone to the governors and complained, so they had insisted that music was given three years to build up its numbers.

The local paper then did it again, with a derogatory article castigating the school, quoting named pupils who had complained about the volume of supply staff they had been receiving due to high rates of staff absence. The pupils had a case. On the same day, I counted sixteen members of staff who needed cover at some time.

We had been moaning for weeks amongst ourselves about losing our free periods to the timetable group of six managers, who met time and time again in the opulent suite at the top of the school, while everyone else had to cover their (admittedly infrequent) lessons. Annoyance was compounded, when the last planned heads of department meeting of the term, and the only remaining opportunity, therefore, to discuss the proposed loss of history to the curriculum at "A" level, as well as the music debacle, was cancelled.

Instead, I went to see the first deputy head to see why she had refused my request to go to my annual "A" level feedback meeting with the exam board. Apart from being an important opportunity to talk to colleagues in other schools, it was the most useful get together in the year, as far as curricular development was concerned. She went on about there being too many people going out and no money left in the budget, which was probably quite right. I made clear that in this particular instance it would only have needed one lesson to be covered. She advised me to try another route, on blue paper this time, to see if the head would wear it if no cover was brought in.

The timetabling saga continued. The governors had apparently told them that they could take nothing off the timetable without providing a year's notice of the change. The part-time bursar, a former deputy, was thought to still have the timetabling brief in his job description, but he no longer performed that role. It was quite mystifying why they had not hauled him on board. Instead, one of their number went to another school to find out how it was done. It used to be one deputy's add-on responsibility, but the six were obviously struggling with it. In the report to the governors, the head said that three members of the senior management team had been on a very successful time-tabling course, with another one due to go in the next term. The only staff meeting set to take place in the summer term was cancelled, because the head was out of school on that day, but it was not rearranged.

The head had been told to put music back on the timetable at both examination levels. She had prevaricated, we were told, over whether this was simply advice to be considered from the governors, or an instruction. It was an instruction. The governors had been stirred into life. The head had been asked about the amount of teaching the senior management did. She allegedly said that she would have to look it up. I could have informed them that the head taught none, the first deputy three and the key stage managers twelve each.

A recent addition to the office staff handed in her resignation, because she was not prepared to be spoken to by a deputy head, "*in that way*". At an event to say goodbye to the caretaker - a stalwart and a good servant to the school in its earlier incarnation - I spoke to the former acting head of the boys' school, in the period prior to amalgamation. We discussed a former head of English, when the school was a grammar school in the 1960s. "*He was a character*", he said. "*Everyone had something about them, then*", he went on. We agreed that probably people still had something about them now, but that it was more difficult to express yourself because the demands on your time were so much greater, whether in fighting for your personal discipline without much back up, meeting the more specific requirements of exam boards or the explosion of paperwork. He went on to say that this guy had also been lazy, but had got away with it. I remembered "characters" at my grammar school, too, some useless and some excellent. People hanker after the "good old days" of the grammar schools, but quite a lot of people got away with doing next to nothing for years. In grammar schools, clever kids sometimes got on in spite of some of their teachers, rather than because of them.

The truly heroic and battling performances were probably being put in at the secondary modern schools down the road, where the forgotten 75% of the cohort went, with fewer resources per child, lower pupil aspirations and more social problems to face. Meanwhile, some weak grammar school teachers - characters or not - drifted along for decades without being rumbled and that was wrong.

The few really weak performers that I had known were either not very well organised souls or those who didn't appear to like children very much. The kids sussed out both types in no time at all and then they really had got a battle on their hands. They said to each other, this person is a waste of space or this person despises us and then they acted accordingly.

The old head had said you couldn't afford to drop your guard nowadays, because if you behaved like yourself or showed kids more aspects of your own personality they would take you to the cleaners, because your ability to keep a grip personally was all you now had to fall back on. In the old days you had the cane. Kids were afraid of stepping out of line and teachers with weaker personal discipline could still rely on it to be administered elsewhere in the building. You also had the very real threat available of kicking them out of a grammar school, which very few of the youngsters would want to countenance even if they were determined to drift. Nor, indeed, would their parents, putting added pressure on them to behave properly.

One of the other former faculty heads confidently predicted that the county inspectorate was going to take a close interest in the management. Meanwhile, all the senior management team, apart from the head, were off on a jolly for the day with the best attenders for the year, amongst the kids. They deserved a break from all that timetabling after all.

The Chief Inspector of Schools was sounding off again and getting government backing for reporting all Ofsted scores to head teachers in an attempt to weed out more of the 15,000 crap teachers there were supposed to be, or was it 150,000 or maybe it was 1,500,000?

It was close to the end of the school year that I witnessed the most remarkable piece of theatre I could remember in my career. The head, late again for morning briefing and hot-foot from the previous day's governors' meeting, made a most vitriolic attack on the governors' decision to insist that both GCSE and "A" level music should run in the next year. This was a barely veiled attack on the head of music herself and on the campaign waged via parent governors, who had children who would have been directly affected by such a decision, to the extent that their withdrawal from the school was a real possibility. A temporary teacher of French, who had been with us for a term and was leaving on that day, refused the farewell presentation the head tried to make to him on the grounds that he was disgusted by what he had just heard. What incredible presence of mind he had exhibited in the process. I'm sure that I would have just held my hand out in stunned silence, had it been me. The head of music and two other staff were refused opportunities to reply.

The head had said that the governors were insisting that the senior management team were to make every endeavour to put on the two music exam courses. She said that the senior management team was unhappy about that, because neither course was viable, as they would have been dealing with only two and four pupils, respectively. She said the fuss over music was the reason nobody had received any timetables, which would otherwise have been ready. She said cuts would have to be made elsewhere to pay for the courses. She implied that no points would be available for teachers while they were having to staff uneconomic courses and that less money would be available for other curriculum areas to buy resources. The overall gist was that she knew there was a campaign to reinstate music and that she was very upset at being over-ruled by the governors. The key practical point was that music and history could easily have been funded if the senior management team took on more teaching.

"Unprecedented" was the word I kept hearing all day, *"In all my twenty-five years teaching..."* and so on, but it was true. A maths teacher said she felt ashamed she had not spoken out. I think everyone felt like that. It was hard to describe the electricity of the occasion. My heart was pounding and I felt a little sweaty across my forehead. If I had had to speak, it might have come out all squeaky, but I still wish I'd said how disgusted I was.

At the well-attended, emergency inter-union meeting after school, a decision was made to ask the head for an apology, to be delivered before the end of term, and also to write a letter to the governors telling them that we rejected the implications the head made and stating that her views were not those of the staff. I offered the meeting my observation that these problems could have been avoided if the head had promoted legitimate opportunities to debate issues openly from the start. The idea that teachers can manipulate parent governors for their own ends was far-fetched. It was in all our interests that not just music and history, but religious education, sociology and chemistry, too, were offered on the timetable at "A" level.

The union representatives went to see the head first thing in the morning with a request for an apology. She asked them to come back again at the end of the school day, when she would have some information for them. They did. She said she would apologise to the staff at the next morning's briefing. At that evening's meeting of the staff, we agreed to listen to the apology but make no comment. We agreed to go ahead with the letter to the governors, which disassociated us from the head's expressed interpretation of the situation.

The letter to the governors was prepared and circulated to staff. It made clear that we wanted to be distanced from the head's views. We complained about the dictatorial manner in which she had delivered them and spoke about our growing lack of confidence in the management of the school.

On the penultimate day of term, we agreed at a meeting of our own union, the National Association of Schoolmasters and Union of Women Teachers, that we would submit an elaboration of our concerns and send them to the governors, as well. We seemed to me to be moving towards a vote of no confidence in our senior management team.

The head apologised in briefing. It was terse, subdued and to the point. She was apologising for the fact that her anger at the governors was misdirected at the staff. The union representatives had been to see her and the letter had gone off to the governors.

One morning at the beginning of the summer holidays, the most popular national tabloid newspaper's banner headline was about our school. A girl in year ten had received her expulsion notice, issued by the head because she had dared to criticise the school in a letter she had written to the local paper, complaining specifically about the number of supply teachers that had been assigned to teach her during her pre-examination year. Her dismissal came about because she had refused to apologise for her actions.

The TV news reckoned that the government were asking for a report on what had been going on. The chairman of the governors spluttered defiance on the lunchtime national news. The Chief Inspector of Schools discussed the wider implications on Newsnight and there was half a page on it in the Guardian. The girl herself appeared to be coming out of it quite well. An amiable looking youngster, well turned out and with her parents' support, reasonable in tone and wisely not over-elaborating on her first few concerns, she made an amazing impact, which was only confirmed by the repeated showings on all the TV news outlets.

Her dad also came across as justifiably aggrieved, concentrating on his right to free speech and democratic participation as a parent. Quite right, too. Unknowingly, he had hit on something which had bugged me for years. The Chief Inspector of Schools said that the girl should not have been punished and that the head should account for her actions. What a turn around. The chairman of the school's governors muttered even less convincingly about institutions not having their members rushing to the press *"willy-nilly"*, but he looked and sounded like a man already floundering out of his depth. The head was branded as a dictator by a national newspaper and the evening paper in the city was talking about an unhappy staff. The local paper was concentrating on the possibility of a staff vote of no confidence. Weeks later, towards the end of August, when I went to school for the GCSE results, there was a TV reporter talking into a camera at the foot of the drive, although it was already well after the precipitous event.

At the start of the autumn term, the press photographed the girl returning to school - with black hair now she was a celebrity, instead of her usual blonde. The media were very much aware of the unsettled nature of our school. We received a message from the head with overtures about a new consultative group to iron out the communications problems that existed between staff and management. We asked for more details, rather than being seen to make a negative response.

The timetable was unveiled, at last. It was a hotchpotch - split classes, classes down for the same subject twice in a day, uncomfortably long 105-minute doubles with year nine classes in academic subjects, teachers finding themselves landed with things they did not expect to have to teach, etc. Some people were talking about rejecting it as unworkable. I spoke against this. It was operable, but just poorly drawn up. I thought it was important that we should not allow ourselves to be portrayed as being in any way provocative. We decided to ask for a meeting to discuss it, which we were granted. At the meeting, the head admitted straight away that it was educationally unsound and announced that the part-time bursar, who had considerable previous experience of timetabling, together with the phase inspector, would start from scratch and provide a new timetable in some weeks. It was a quick meeting. I didn't know how the senior management team's timetable group members could even look us in the face. All those lessons they granted themselves away from their classes during the previous term whilst others covered for them and it had culminated in an unworkable mess that the head had agreed was a disaster. We were asked, as heads of department, to resubmit our original requirements and inform her of any changes we wished to make, so they could start straight away.

The head of science was still furious, claiming that a member of the senior management team, who was also a science teacher as well as being a member of the timetabling group, had changed his departmental staff allocation submission (an important and unambiguous part of his role) to give themselves sixth form teaching only. The head had apparently attempted to explain this to him as just a clash of personalities.

There was a steady flow of information to the press by then and we had been on local TV and radio again, even providing material for Radio Four's "Thought for the Day" about communication - or a lack of it, presumably, in our case.

The head of history, in his calm and measured way, polite and reasonable as ever, had been trying to put a bit of pressure on about the restoration to the timetable of his subject at advanced level, now that we were supposedly starting afresh. The head side-stepped it, saying it needed the head of the governor's approval.

Meanwhile, a senior management team member was reported as having advised a potential "A" level history student to go to the technical college to enrol there, instead of staying on at school. I then lost a promising geography candidate because he was so disgusted with the lack of interest shown in him on his first day in the sixth form. I was told that this included the failure of a member of the senior management team to turn up to his first "A" level biology session. No doubt somewhat perplexed, as well as legitimately annoyed, he also left on that day and walked down and signed on at the local technical college.

The information technology man, who taught a bit of geography and had hardly poked his nose above the parapet until then, claimed that he had been threatened with disciplinary proceedings if he failed to deliver, by putting right immediately a missed deadline for a piece of administration. He had always kept things to himself beforehand, but by then even he felt able to splutter his grievance publicly. Everything was very fluid, but the kids, of course, continued to be predictably loud and excitable about the place.

The new French teacher was so put off by non-committal responses to her *"What if I have trouble in the classroom?"* questions, that she went straight to the head at the end of the day and told her she would not be coming back. In doing so, she joined the ever-lengthening list of people who may well have been very talented and have had something to offer under normal circumstances, but who had been driven away by our version of reality.

As subject managers, we usually received our staff deployment sheets prior to the start of each academic year. It was in the form of a matrix that already indicated which staff would be contributing to the department and how many lessons each teacher would be teaching within it.

That was the timetable person's job, resulting, no doubt, from their previous discussions with the management.

My initial submission was suddenly returned to me unchanged, and I was asked to resubmit it. Out of the blue, I had a visit from the head, saying she would like to teach a year nine geography class. I said that though I welcomed her offer to contribute to the department, my assistant was already expecting to take that class. My former middle school assistant teacher had expertise in the lower school but lacked experience in the upper school at examination level. I was summoned to speak with the secondary phase inspector, who said it would be good to make use of the head's expertise as a geographer. I said I would have a word with the teacher who would be affected by the head taking up one of her classes. She was not happy about it at all. Geography was her first subject and she would rather be doing that than anything else. The form was returned to me again. This time, the head's name had been added. I told the second deputy head, also in my department, that I was not happy about that. He said put it in writing. I wrote that if the head was going to do geography it should be in year ten and at the expense of the historian who taught a bit of geography, or a special needs colleague who did the same. Neither had been involved with geography until relatively recently and both had their specialisms elsewhere.

Up to this point, my one-to-one relations with the head and all the senior managers had been courteous and professional and I did not want that to change, in spite of all the other issues that made life difficult for me. I knew that my intransigence would be interpreted as (at best) uncooperative, but it was time to make a stand, even if my personal relationship with the head was to become strained. As I saw it, the head had been told that she had got to do some teaching at last, and that she would be doing it because she had been left no choice. I went back to the head. She said that losing one class out of four would not weaken my assistant's contribution to the department and that the historian with a bit of left-over time for geography would have been happy to take a year ten class instead. I said it would be the other year ten class that she (the head) would be down to take, which would otherwise be staffed by the special needs man and the information technology specialist between them. She said that would leave the information technology man's timetable light if he were not to do it.

I walked straight out from seeing the head into a meeting with the secondary phase inspector. I told him what I had said to the head. He said he would speak to her and get back to me. I bumped into the head again and she called me in. I told her I was supporting my assistant geographer, trying to protect her interests and making what I considered to be the right decision for my department. I wanted to maximise my colleague's exposure to year nine, where she had always been successful in attracting a high proportion of each cohort to opt for geography in year ten. I said that if people senior to me made decisions to overturn my submission, then I would have no control over it. We went over the whole thing again, and in the end, I said I was simply repeating myself. The head saw that I was not going to change my mind, so she ended the conversation. Though formal and polite on the surface, it was strained and stressful as well. She knew that I had always fitted in previously but I dug my heels in and I did not let my assistant down. I had discussed the same issue with senior staff and inspectors six times in two days. The secondary phase inspector said he would ask the head why she would not take a year ten class and then let me know.

In briefing the next day, we received deployment sheets yet again. I returned mine to the second deputy head at lunchtime, as requested, with no changes made. The secretary asked me to contact the secondary phase inspector urgently. He said he would probably put the head down for some teaching time in geography. The head had made it clear that if she did not have a year nine class, she did not want anything. I stuck rigidly to my position. In protecting the interests of my staff, I might have ended up letting the head off the teaching hook. I guessed that she wouldn't have minded that at all, had the phase inspector decided not to over-rule me and he wasn't able to find her anything else to do.

The more I turned it over in my head, the more I felt that I was being manipulated. I never received a sheet clearly saying that the head would have two or three lessons, or whatever. The final version had her name at the top of a column but still no indication of the number of lessons to fill in on her behalf. It felt like, for reasons unknown, somebody senior to me wanted me to climb down without actually telling me that I had to. I was effectively being asked rather vaguely what was I going to do about the head, to which my answer was "Nothing". If I had been told how many lessons of geography she was going to teach, I would have exercised my legitimate role and deployed her as I saw fit, no problem. However, it felt as though extraneous pressure was being put on me to make a decision outside of my brief, because it was easier for other people to do it that way. I stood my ground and my initial deployment remained unchanged.

The head of science (and former faculty head) told me his doctor was on the verge of advising him to have two months off with stress-related illness and to stay at home and do nothing. My colleague said he no longer had any appetite for the fight. He was a strong personality and we needed him on board, but I told him nothing was worth risking his health for. Perhaps health was now clearly the bottom line for me as well.

I had never felt so depressed about school as I did after my results meeting with the head and the head of the sixth form in late September 1997. The reason, on the face of it, was obvious, bad results and my fault. The second deputy head did well with both his sets. He was very steady, even, apparently, when he was not even there for a lot of the time. My second set also did marginally better than average, which in itself was little short of miraculous, given that they were a largely disinterested and alienated bunch wherever they went. The problem was in my third set. It was clear to me from the outset that I had collected a right group there, who had somehow managed through native wit and certainly not examination revision, to score sufficiently highly in their year nine tests to find their way into my set rather than the bottom one. Ten out of the thirty were either downright disruptive or with serious learning difficulties, or both. This was the worst class I'd had for years. I could not get them to listen to me. I gave up. I contained them. I did not chase up their truancy. I shut the door, provided them with work to do and prevented them damaging the room or each other as best I could for two years. I predicted disastrous results and that is what I got. The special needs guy's set also did badly. He had a right collection in there.

I told the head all this in acceptable language and I was honest, up to a point, about my disappointment and about my limitations in not getting enough out of them. History had gained most of the academic kids at fourteen plus in that cohort, which was also reflected in their results (18 A-C grades against our 11). This was in spite of the fact that we attracted 5 full classes of geographers to two for history. In other words, we had a really bottom-heavy cohort and it showed, leaving us three quarters of the way down the departmental list of successes. It was depressing to know that I had failed many of the kids in this bad class. It upset me to admit that I had run out of energy and effectively washed my hands of a few nice kids, who consequently under-achieved. I wish I could have diverted my disappointment into the anger I had felt on other occasions, but I had to carry the blame personally as well.

We were soon to be inundated with inspectors – local education authority quality assurance the following Friday, the local education authority again the week after that and then HMI, as well, only days later. The inspections would be thorough and follow a set pattern. They would be dispassionate and consistent in their approach. There was nowhere to hide. Teacher, plus room, plus resources, plus kids, equalled results. You could only dress things up so much. As a school we deserved to be put on the spot. I tried to resolve to show that I was still a strength and not a weakness.

That one class had dented my confidence massively and had drawn attention to my department for the first time, at the wrong time and in the wrong way. We had never been below average before, in my memory. I had always been associated with successful departments throughout my teaching life. I had to show them that this was just a blip.

It hurt more, deep down, because I knew very well that the situation described was not all my fault. I lost faith in the management's propensity and willingness to help me in difficult situations years before. I shut my door on the rest of the school in the previous year because I had effectively been told that if I needed help, I was a failure. I resolved to manage by myself so as not to draw attention to my shortcomings, to have them recognised as such or to be branded officially as failing. That was not how it should have been.

On the penultimate day of inspections, we got told off again for walking past fighting in the quad which was witnessed by the local education authority's humanities inspector, yet the management were only out there themselves when there was an inspection on. Both the local education authority inspectors and HMI asked us specifically about management. They were told the truth pretty openly, too.

In mid-October, our union representative told us that the governors would soon have the two reports from the inspectors to go on and they would have to choose a course of action. We had certainly strayed into the subject of management at the quality assurance feedback meeting with the local education authority's humanities inspector. I told him about my difficult bottom set, thirty on the role, including ten trouble makers and one of them up on an attempted manslaughter charge. I said it was just a matter of containment, protecting the room and trying to keep people happy. I told him I had lost faith in the management's ability to help me. The only member of the senior management team who had the authority at that time to be of any help to me was also teaching at the same time and was therefore unavailable. I said that I had consequently felt very isolated. The inspector was a bit obscure at that point, saying that he knew some things that he was not able to divulge at that point in time. There was no reference to our discussion in his written report.

I also had a chat with an HMI inspector. He had watched me with a year ten class for twenty-five minutes without comment the day before, though he wrote notes all the time. He then had a whole year 13 lesson with me and asked to see all the administration, as well - departmental handbook, lesson plans, schemes of work, pre-Ofsted reports, Ofsted reports, quality assurance reports and other departmental business. We went into their base room. As with the local education authority man, he gave little away. He said it was clear from the paperwork that I was moving forward with post-Ofsted issues and involving the department in the required processes. I said I was self-motivated and that I knew which directions I wanted to go in. He asked what constraints there were which hampered progress and I said discipline. I said we did not get enough support from the senior management team and that they were not always on patrol in the way that they were now. I told him about the hypocrisy of our being admonished for not challenging incidents, whilst they appeared to make it their life's work, it seemed to me, to avoid confrontation with kids. I let him know of my contempt for this attitude without actually saying so. The bell went and he told me to go and get a cup of tea. I felt elated that I had not let the opportunity to get things off my chest pass me by.

The asbestos in my classroom ceiling was to be removed over half term. The two reports to the governors were due. Potentially powerful and dangerous stuff - all three, in fact.

A couple of days later, the head and the chairman of the governors met with HMI. The report's contents were devastating. We had failed and would be put into special measures. 40% of lessons were unsatisfactory and management was poor. It was difficult to take any pleasure in their findings, though it was impossible not to feel at least partly vindicated.

During the last two days before the October half term holiday, the head was not in school. There was a buzz of excitement amongst colleagues, but suppressed, just below the surface, expecting that something big was going to happen. We were informed that the head man from the local education authority would address us at briefing on the first day back after half term. My guess was that the head had been offered a passage out and might have been granted time to think about any proposal that had been made to her. The first deputy head had not been in school for two weeks by the end of that half of term.

On the 3rd of November 1997, we were informed that the head had resigned. The kids were told in assembly and were as high as kites all day. An acting head was appointed, an inspector with the local authority. He looked powerful and assertive, but was likely to be with us only for one and a half terms. We were on telly again - the BBC national news at lunchtime and two spots on PM on Radio Four, as well as in the national newspapers.

We were then just ticking over, waiting for a new action plan. It was all behind the scenes stuff. Some staff thought it was somewhat galling, however, to see the fringe members of the senior management team in there with the new team as if nothing had happened. One of them was standing outside the loos between lessons. That must have been a first, I mused. The smell was appalling - from the loos, I mean.

The newly appointed teacher governors returned with half a year's worth of governors' meetings' minutes which had mysteriously failed to appear since the time of the music dispute. The gem from the collection was the revelation that the first deputy head had walked out of the meeting in which she was over-ruled by the governors on the issue.

Another representative from the local education authority (they were certainly well staffed down there) outlined preparations for special measures and gave us copies of their report, which made fascinating reading. Basically, it vindicated our position, held for all these years and it roundly condemned the performance of the senior management team. The acting head prepared us for a right fuss with the press over the coming days with the publication of the HMI report.

Some of us had been battling for this recognition for three years but now we had won. Those with ultimate power and authority had come out and backed our view of the world. What a great shame, I thought, that no-one had listened when we had started to point out what was wrong to the chair of governors and to our phase inspector. It was clear, however, that the higher level of scrutiny that we had become used to was going to continue. We hoped that what would come out of it would be a better school, better behaved kids, a happier working environment and the knowledge that we were working in a place which was on the up.

That seemed to be an appropriate time to take stock. I was appointed as head of faculty from 1993, a role I held until 1995. I relished the potential chance to influence things that it had granted me. Two years on, the faculty system had been abandoned and I had been demoted on the grounds of scarce resources and a top-heavy management structure. We suspected that it was really because by that time, as a group of four heads of faculty, we had already become the focal point of opposition to the head, her management style and the policy changes that had been brought in that we wanted to question. This campaign culminated in a letter to the chairman of governors which summarised our grievances and was never replied to. Instead, we were admonished by our leader for going above her head and made to apologise, as well as agreeing to a loyalty clause. Our objections were clear cut. The heads of faculty were expected to teach a full timetable, run their faculties, run their departments, be form tutors, take their turns on yard duty and the on-call system, be responsible for discipline in their faculty to the extent that if a faculty member needed direct assistance in their teaching situation, they were to interrupt the head of faculty as the first port of call. It was then the heads of faculty's duty to chase up the attendant paperwork for the incident and run any follow-up punishment systems, like a faculty detention, that they considered to be necessary. There was, at first, no school detention system. This was only won begrudgingly from the senior management team towards the end of that period. The withdrawal room (sin bin), which the heads of faculty also had to contribute to staffing, was over-subscribed (hardly surprising, under the circumstances) and was discontinued in 1995 because after further swingeing staff reductions we were told that it could not adequately be manned. As heads of faculty, we had been at our wits' end. Whilst we had everything to do, the head taught nothing - for four years as it turned out. The deputy's teaching commitment shrank from 5 lessons to 2 per week. What I had found particularly upsetting was that we let our phase inspector, our life-line to the outside world, know all this. He even asked us to convey our thoughts to the local education authority's pre-Ofsted inspection teams, which we did, but to no avail. He must surely have felt a bit embarrassed about it all eventually. If he had acted at the time that he was told, he could surely have prevented our having to suffer this damage to the school and its pupils. I guess they would say they did not have the evidence then, but I felt that they were actually very slow to take us seriously, even though the senior management team were eventually discredited.

There was more media coverage about the local education authority's report. We were informed that we were to contribute to working groups, so that all points in the new action plan could be addressed in time, so it looked like a lot of work was coming our way. With at least six staff off sick, there were new supply teachers in school all the time and the mean streets of the cloisters were probably as under-patrolled as ever. One lady visitor said she had been on the receiving end of the worst bout of swearing she had ever faced in her thirty-year career.

We were allocated to chair working groups and I was given the quality of teaching one to deal with (Are you sure?). What I really needed was some time and energy to address some new classroom activities. I felt sorry for the head of special needs. He had been slated in the HMI report. If there was one person who did not deserve that, then it was him. Without him, the place would have imploded during the previous couple of years. He fielded all of life's problem children with a smile. Meanwhile the paperwork kept on coming. However, the acting head had the natural bearing of a man who really believed he could do it.

Although we had five long term absentees, we were keeping our free periods rather more, so the supply teachers must have been arriving in a regular stream. The kids' behaviour was still awful, though, and I lost it for a few minutes chasing a lad from my dreadful tutor group round the cloisters and into a room, before yanking him out by his coat. He said he was going home, but I saw him later drifting round school doing pretty much as he pleased and then being pulled out of class by someone else. I wrote a referral and sent it straight to the management team because I had touched him. That was not something you would have chosen to do if you sat down and thought about it. His outer garment was somewhat on the grubby side. The lad got all his kudos from being naughty. It was the only way he got any attention from those in his class, who had an unhealthy, dismissive contempt for him the rest of the time. He was derided and bullied. I got so frustrated with his defiance that I snapped for a moment - dangerous, but understandable.

The acting head, and the henchman he brought with him, were gradually realising the scale of the problems, first hand. Apparently, the same boy had given the head's new number two the run-around, running away and hiding round corners from him. The day before, one of the special needs teacher's lads had pushed the guy in the chest and the boy had been excluded at a stroke.

We were still unable to ignore or under-estimate the influence of our recent local history. The company that had taken over the remaining coal mines in the wider area had announced even more closures and redundancies. I saw real resentment in the faces of our kids. It was as if they understood the essence of their collective lot in life and they hated it. I wrote that they had seemed to be drunk on bad behaviour and that it had spread to kids who had not previously become infected. I didn't think that I had ever been so tired before, by that stage in the term. In the end, the most traumatic and taxing term in my life just petered out. By Christmas, I was knackered. For the first time ever, I took no work home to address during the holiday. I really needed a rest.

On our return, at the beginning of January 1998, we were expecting a new permanent head to have been appointed on the first day, but the white smoke had not risen by the time I left for home. Before the end of the month, however, the new head had been announced and immediate reactions were favourable. He introduced himself at morning briefing and I first spoke to him at the sixth form parents' evening. He was to start in April. Prior to that, the acting head had already announced that an assessment of roles would take place. He had chosen his words carefully. Did he mean a complete re-structuring? We would have to wait and see.

The acting head's dogsbody came to see my year eleven top set lesson and said it was *"Excellent"*. I said it was fairly straightforward with a good class. He said that when I had my forthcoming interview in connection with the re-assessment of roles, I should tell the truth. I said of course I would. He emphasised that he meant I should openly tell the truth. A little perplexed, I said that I would do that, too.

My chat with the phase inspector that followed was a complete waste of time. It was just a re-run of what had happened before. He asked me slightly veiled questions about relationships between the senior management team and the rest of the staff. He jumped on everything I said that had been mildly contentious, rephrased it, strengthening the criticism as he went, and then asked me if it was still OK. I said, *"Sure"*. Then he wrote it down. I approved what he had written and we left it at that.

On the 4th of March, we were informed that the schools' minister would visit school on Monday 30th. At the same time, we were advertising nationally for a replacement deputy head. New plans were gradually unfolding and we learnt that curriculum and pastoral responsibilities were now to be split, just like in the old days. To suggest such a thing during the years immediately preceding this time, was to be assured of a good "poo-pooing". It struck me how frequently some things in education come around again eventually, if you stuck around long enough to witness them. The new hierarchy would be expected to teach for substantial chunks, we were told, also against the prevailing tide elsewhere, I would have suggested.

By early April 1998, the interregnum was over. He was an imposing figure but on the day that he left at the end of that term there were about fifteen kids down for detention and nobody had turned up. That was a really big deal and indicative of sustained and deeply engrained problems, but no-one felt like spoiling the party, or maybe no-one had any appetite left for a fight. We would have to get to grips with problems like that if we were going to make progress. The new head had a lot of goodwill waiting for him and a lot of crossed fingers. The minister postponed his visit. Perhaps he had thought a bit longer and harder about whether it would have been a really good day out, after all.

I needed to send a letter home to the household whence came the girl who precipitated the fall of the old regime. Her younger brother could be quite an annoying little chap. I wrote to his parents to complain about his behaviour. I briefly had second thoughts about whether I should send it, because of what had gone before. I sure as hell needed to send it. To send the other letters I had prepared and not to send his would hardly have been fair. I sent it. It actually struck me how disruptive he was when he was then absent for a week and the class was so much better without him.

The new head spoke well to the staff at his first assembly and was visible around the school. At the staff meeting, he said they had shortlisted 13 for the deputy's job and they hoped to be able to appoint two deputies by the time of the interviews. HMI had announced their intention to visit us, though a "light touch" inspection was promised, whatever that meant.

It turned out that the HMI was a former geographer and once worked for the examination board. I had met him through subject meetings but he would not have remembered me. He tiptoed around school wearing an unconvincing smile. I was inspected for five minutes of registration. I got them all in the room, they sat down, they answered their names, some of them even said "*Sir*" in reply. I won, hands down. He carried on smiling and then left - quietly.

I got the feedback from the head. He said lots of year nine lessons that they had seen were unsatisfactory, but they could see we were moving in the right direction. Literacy, social interaction and poor listening skills were highlighted. I was fuming. I said to the head that we get them at thirteen years of age. They have been all the way through two schools by the time they get to us. If we were to blame for all that, what about the role of the primary and middle schools? When were they going to get down there and sort them out? I suppose it was a bit of a rant, really, whilst at the same time I was trying not to be impolite to the new boss.

We were told that we all had to apply for our own jobs yet again. At the same time as we were trying to profess progress, positivism, togetherness and self-belief to our new leader, he was doing his best to brainwash us into thinking that things were getting better. They were not. The day before, a lad set fire to the boys' toilets - the paper and the loo-roll holder, primarily. The smell of burning plastic was luckily tracked down by the workmen who were putting in the nearby equal opportunities lift.

I was interviewed for the new (re-instated) head of faculty post against the head of history. I got the job again, for the second time in five years. Again, he bore me no grudge. He was always decent to me and it was much appreciated. By the last day of term, I realised that I had amazingly managed 100% attendance throughout, but I was still not invited to go on the day out that the good attenders received as their reward. The new head held a good assembly. He had made a sound start. He looked tough, if a little self-satisfied, very confident in his own ability and maybe with a bit of a ruthless streak. I generally felt a bit more optimistic.

During the summer holidays in 1998, I was buoyed up by my best ever GCSE results - 4 "A*s" and nine at "A". I wondered if that entitled me to wise elder statesman role, revered figure, past glories, all that accumulated know how? Almost certainly not. You were only as good as your last set of results so I had got a year of feeling I was a bit of a smart-arse and then it would be back to the usual excuses. I hoped that the new head was not going to praise me publicly in a staff meeting like the previous incumbent had done over the "A2" level results two years previously. The truth of the matter was that the results were better because the year group doing geography was better and they were likely to fall again immediately because the next two years were weaker by comparison - and then it would be my fault. I kept on noticing that the head was good at making the right noises. I kept on finding myself saying, yes, I would have said that if I was in his position. I expected him to fight a good media battle on our behalf.

The new regime had some early success and by half term, absenteeism was down, so my unsettled classes were bulging with naughty children. I had experienced a bad week, confrontationally speaking, and had hoped that it was not the re-start of the seemingly perpetual battle over disaffection and discipline that had led to divisions of opinion previously between pastoral and curricular areas.

A naughty boy was throwing berries around that he had picked from a bush outside my classroom. In the process, he brought a whole new meaning to the term harvest festival. He chucked them at the others in the class periodically throughout the lesson, so at the end I told him to stay and pick up the mess. He promptly walked out. I gave him a detention for disobedience. The next day, there he was again in my lesson, still throwing berries. I sent for on call. The head arrived. I explained the story so far. The head then asked the boy to leave the room with him. The boy stayed put and refused to budge. We all had to leave the room, instead. The head eventually took the boy away and we returned to the classroom. The head brought him back with an apology. The head reminded the boy that he was to do his detention. The boy had already told me that he did not do detentions. The boy did not turn up for my detention. I sent a memo to get the boy into school detention, instead. I sent a memo telling the head where I was up to with it. There was no reply from the head. The boy then went off absent. I remembered hearing from the educational welfare officer once about how rubbish this boy's home life was, but what was I to do? Did I say OK, because you have such a lousy deal at home, we will let you do what you want while you are here? Here, let me help you collect some more berries.

The head's weekly message in the bulletin read like the manager's page in a football programme, full of anodyne platitudes. Perhaps that was how he liked to see himself, being a big football man himself.

Another curious character, who I did not even teach, had, out of nowhere it seemed, taken to calling me "*Shit-pants*", from a distance but within my hearing, whenever he saw me around the place. I had heard bad reports about both lads from three other members of staff, so it was not just me - always reassuring, that. The berries lad, on one of his more communicative days, told me that he had recently gone back to live with his mother, who, he announced, "*is a schizophrenic*".

It was always a risk when you took our lot out of school on field work expeditions. I did it because it was good geography, because I believed in the importance of the coursework component in the GCSE exam and because it was good for them on all sorts of levels to sample something new and different. I did not do field work for a day out for myself. There were lots of things to consider and it was a massive responsibility, especially when you went to a very public place.

It all went pear-shaped at a visit to a reservoir and visitors' centre in the neighbouring county. I knew that we had been noticed for the wrong reasons and I had already apologised to the centre staff for some general rowdiness. I had had to reprimand a group who had taken out two rowing boats, expressly contradicting instructions from me. These kids were fifteen and sixteen. You couldn't march them around holding hands in a crocodile all day. They all had clipboards and set tasks to complete and the boards probably came in handy as makeshift oars, in this instance. Admittedly, the set tasks probably got a soaking and most were possibly clogging up the surrounding area's water supply for ages afterwards. We were quickly followed back to school by a letter from the centre manager saying that she had noted in her diary that we were a *"problem school"* and listing a series of transgressions that had not specifically been mentioned to me on the day, including *"smoking in the toilets, playing with a football in the building, abusing the passenger lift* (I'm not sure how they had done that and she had not gone into any detail) *and eating in the shops"*. She had over-egged it massively. It was a culture clash to be sure, but some people were on the look-out for trouble even before it occurred. Our kids were naturally noisy and were sometimes lacking in social niceties. If challenged the wrong way, their instinct was to respond aggressively. You could tell that was what they were often used to in their daily lives at home and in their community. Situations ratcheted upwards with surprising speed. You had to know how to talk to them, so that problems did not escalate. I wrote a grovelling letter back to the centre. I took multiple field trips in each year for over a quarter of a century with no incidents of anything like that magnitude having happened before, so I wasn't going to be put off by this particular debacle either.

November 8th was the eve of another HMI visit. It would be the quiet one again. Everybody was in a flap. *"It's all a game"*, I said, to anyone who stopped moving long enough to look as though they were listening to me. The feeling was that they were coming for special needs this time. They could be going to follow around some of our more vulnerable pupils. It would be interesting for them to see what a poor deal they got, on a regular basis. Two boys I had in mind were like communal punch bags for other kids' grouses and ill-temper. The kids thought it was perfectly OK to give them a good spontaneous smack out of nowhere when they passed them on the corridor.

Would I be meeting their special educational needs on the next day? No. Would I be able to prevent them suffering verbal abuse? No. Would I be able to stop them being assaulted? No, unless I could get myself between them and their aggressors, like a human shield, in the right place at the right time and even then, only because I had read the signs and moved swiftly. *"It doesn't matter, sir"*, the perpetrators would say, *"It's only Kevin"*. Yes, it did matter, but what the hell could I do about it? Kevin had to survive and cut his own niche. He almost certainly had to do it without my help or anybody else's for most of the time. It was a jungle out there.

The scurrying around for HMI continued. Decrees were issued, paperwork demands made and new initiatives up and running. It hid nothing. The kids were still the same. Behaviour was still appalling. I heard that a gun (air pistol?) was confiscated the week before and in a separate incident, a teacher was accused of assault. I bet that HMI did not hear about either event.

Both the new deputies looked exhausted already and even the super-cool new head was getting a bit ratty. The pressure was building because of the lack of exclusions. They had to be reduced because we were being measured on them, too, just like absences. The trouble was that when kids had been through all the available sanctions and only exclusion was left, they were then just fed back into the system. That weakened the class teachers' available strategies, giving the kids the OK to continue to misbehave and that led to the old pressure cooker situation. With no safety valve, you could easily then get a scenario developing when a less experienced member of staff decided to take the law into his or her own hands, or they simply just flipped, because of the stress they were under.

We were told that we had to do little numeracy and literacy tasks in form period. Not a bad idea, at all. I was thinking of doing one on table football (involving the nudging or flicking of coins), as my class seemed to want to do little else in form period. It encouraged eye/hand coordination, improved dexterity, involved simple maths (score keeping) and cooperation (social skills). I thought about writing it up formally, especially if I was told that it was not a suitable activity for form period.

I got hacked off with the obsession with uniformity thing. It grated with me. Why couldn't I just get on with it in my own way? If there was mayhem or I was calling for help every five minutes, I would have understood, but by and large, I didn't have to. I was finding some classes very difficult, but I preferred to deal with things in my own way as often as possible. If I couldn't manage, I would ask for help. Why did everyone have to try to be the same? This did not teach them about the real world, in which things and people are different. Should they not have been learning this as a priority? The argument was that they can't cope with conflicting messages. That would be to underestimate them. In our day, teachers were all refreshingly different from each other in style, at least. It was part of the interest of the daily diet. That is how people are. Why should we be afraid of letting them know how different people are in the real world? You could get away with some things with some teachers and not with others. It was ever thus. I accepted the challenge on those terms, knowing that some kids got away with some things with me, too. I had a bottom line, as well. I also knew when I needed help. My say so as a professional and as a judge of such things should have been the only deciding factor.

There was another issue there. In one of the new documents for the management of the quiet room, which was the sin bin under another new name and sometimes something of a misnomer, anyway, depending on how many were in there at any one time (when naughty friends from different classes could meet up for further potential mutual entertainment), mention was made of hearing the pupil's point of view in a dispute. Why? We were talking about professional judgements here, about challenging poor behaviour, not an argument between two possibly correct points of view. We may have been equals as fallible human beings, yes, of course, but the roles we had responsibility for couldn't be described as equal in the same way. We should always have been respectful in our dealings with kids, naturally, but that did not mean negotiating with them at every stage. As teachers, in the end we had to do what our head asked us to do even if we disagreed with it. In the same way, the kids had to do what we wanted them to do, otherwise we couldn't operate as an institution.

I blotted my copy book twice in one day. I got caught out by the inspector when my year 13 class were 6 minutes late to my lesson. As a result, my lesson was marked as unsatisfactory. Secondly, there was a purge on wearing coats in class and I got found out by the then recently appointed assistant deputy head whilst on her rounds, when she came into the room to ask my kids to remove their coats. I always told kids to take their coats off, except for the five minutes of p.m. registration, where it would have taken all of that time to get 100% compliance and I would never have got the register done. Anyway, it transpired that the head was going to talk more formally to individual staff who had a problem with it, so I was expecting an invitation to see him.

Then I had a nasty incident when I had to help a lad, who had chosen to walk across the desk tops, back down to ground level. I suppose I gave him a helping hand a bit more abruptly than I should have done. I resolved to keep my cool rather better the next day. Sometimes I got a gut feeling that I was in the wrong place. I should have been in Summerhill, or somewhere similar, because of the apparent obsession with regimentation and uniformity. The supposition was that we had to go through this pain to reach a better place. Time would tell. I resolved to do what I was asked to do, but I was emotionally uncomfortable with a lot of it. There was no evidence at that point that it was making school a happier place. As a girl in my class said to the head the day before, after a frank exchange of views, no doubt, *"I might as well just fuck off home, then"*. I felt a bit like that myself sometimes.

At our meeting after school for the year ten tutors, the special needs man suggested sweat shirts should be part of the uniform. I was all for that if it meant that I didn't have to pick an argument with ten people in my class each morning over uniform, before I even started teaching. I was on call the previous day and summoned to a class where there was a bit of bother. A girl said, *"Why have they sent you, sir, you are too soft?"* I had to agree with her. She was absolutely right. At least she called me sir, I thought, on my way back to the staff room, having sorted out the problem to everyone's apparent satisfaction.

There was disquiet as we approached the holiday. A female member of staff had been hit in the face by a book thrown at her by a pupil and her glasses were broken. The head of science, meanwhile, was hit and cut above the eye by a flying glue stick, launched at him by a girl in year eleven. What will happen to them, we wondered?

I was informed that I had to tell a colleague (nobody else apparently wanted to) that a lesson when the inspector had been present was graded as unsatisfactory. It was a hurtful thing to have to say to a highly regarded and seasoned professional and it upset me, too. This was someone who always demanded high standards of work and behaviour from the pupils. There was no redress from this judgement and no further explanation was forthcoming. I was given no details to pass on and no advice about what needed to change. Decisions like that - the difference between a lesson seen to be just one side of the satisfactory line or the other must often have hung by a thread, yet could be a devastating condemnation if you were judged to have teetered over the edge. How were such borderline decisions made? It had got to be arbitrary. If it went the right way, it would not attract any further attention from anyone. If it went the wrong way, it could have a devastating effect on the individual concerned.

My colleague was first into school every morning, an hour before lessons started, and was a steady, reliable, knowledgeable and thoughtful member of staff. Exercise books were marked assiduously and syllabuses up-dated. There was nobody on the staff who was more aware of the impact of the children's reading levels on their ability to learn. Though not the only one who had been marked out for criticism, I was not even permitted to pass on that information.

This issue went straight back to the politics of it all. Measuring schools' progress against each other meant increased polarisation. Polarisation meant more pressure on the schools that served poorer areas. We responded in that most deprived of areas as best we could. It really got to me. I was fed up of being blamed. We often taught wild, distressed or neglected children. We were expected to be substitutes for parents - for ineffectual parents, for disinterested parents, for violent parents or for those simply lacking parenting skills - no doubt, in some cases, as their parents had done before them. We were pilloried for doing a good job in difficult circumstances, because our good job was not enough to paper over the massive division in society between the newly expanded and aspiring middle-class and large sections of the working-class rump who were increasingly left behind on the estates.

Then we had the go-ahead for an 11 to 18 school and the abolition of the middle schools and further disruption. How could we possibly turn this round, so that we would become a school that discriminating parents for whom there was a realistic choice - because they were wealthy enough, articulate enough or interested enough to have a positive say in the matter - would want to send their kids?

The new head still gave the impression of being very cool under all this pressure. If he was to pull it off, he would certainly have earned himself a reputation. Generally, people wished him well and were reluctant to take him to task over anything. This was because he had a generally positive manner about him and because no-one wanted to be seen as rocking the boat, for the time being, at least. Yet, on the same day, a dinner lady was assaulted, described as having her arm pulled out of its socket by a year nine boy. There was a lot of pushing and shoving in the dining hall and the dinner ladies asked for extra help. I went in to see if I could be of use. It was chaotic in there. I don't think I could have stayed that long. A short period of respite at lunch time remained critical.

We heard that the head had not given support to a member of staff who had used an arm to restrain a boy who, it was claimed, had lashed out and made contact. The head went by the book and suspended the teacher on full pay. Apparently, the police were involved, but the story was that the staff member had been cleared alongside an offer of reinstatement, which, unsurprisingly, was refused. That was somebody else lost to us who had been happy to have a go under difficult circumstances, though perhaps "having a go" was not the most appropriate way to put it in this particular instance.

I was asked to offer *"expert tuition"* to a colleague with a problematic class during the last lesson of the day. (Was someone taking the Mickey?) During the time I was away from my own lesson, where a supply teacher had briefly stood in for me, one lad stormed out, had a wander round, then went back in again. I could see all this from the place that I had been sent to. When I went back there at the end of the lesson the supply teacher said, *"That lot were unbearable"*. The kids told me later that the teacher had called James a *"spaz"* and James had told the supply teacher to *"Fuck off, you grey haired twat"*. So that was all sorted, then.

The county's humanities inspector, was in again. He told a teacher of religious education that a lesson he had witnessed was poor and that official monitoring would then follow. This was not altogether a surprise to me.

An enabling document to accompany local education authority plans to do away with the three-tier system of education in the town was announced in January 1999. Our catchment area was to stay the same. In short, we were going to be left with the poorest end of town again. The head's weekly pep talks in the staff bulletin looked increasingly desperate to me, as though we were being encouraged to fight relegation for the third year running in a "backs to the wall" last few games of the season. Could we escape from special measures in the allotted time? Nothing much had changed and it was still very hard graft.

The former second deputy head had returned to my department. He had been quite critical, bringing up various things he thought that I'd got wrong or overlooked. I did not quite understand what his problem was. He told me that he had a loose screw. I tried not to look surprised and he then said it was in his leg, following his recent knee operation. It would require further time off school for him, which would obviously mean more supply cover to deal with for me.

The paperwork overload continued. We had to feed back to the head with our evaluations of the literacy initiatives we had made during the last term. I found this mildly insulting. I had always consistently tried to initiate improvements on a regular basis and it was a real pain having to justify what you have always known was the right thing to do, like you were not being trusted to try to make progress of your own volition. I decided to get a bit smarter on that one, by feeding back stuff that reflected changes I had already planned to make, if not actually made beforehand. Why did we have to go through this lengthy administrative charade just to identify a few lazy people? We all knew who they were already.

My colleague in the room next door had virtually no discipline problems and we all benefited from his return, because our neck of the woods had been noticeably quieter all week, without the procession of supply teachers. He achieved good results for his kids, year in year out, yet he had tried nothing new as far as curriculum development was concerned, all the time that I had worked with him, as far as I was aware. He would have argued that he did not have to and he would have had a point. I just thought about what I could have done additionally if I had had his discipline, as well. My system worked well for biddable, brighter, hard-working kids, but fell down with those who lacked their own self-discipline and those that had to share the room with them. We are what we are. I was trapped in my own personality. I couldn't re-invent myself. I had thought about early retirement more than once around this time. "I am only 49, for heaven's sake", I had muttered to myself. At what stage would people start talking about me as dead wood?

In March, the new deputy invited me to inaugurate Part One, Leisure and Tourism, in the new General National Vocational Qualification initiative aimed at the non-academic kids.

The head was assured that we would come out of special measures, but I didn't know by whom. We had to continue to have written evidence of having planned every lesson and these would be spot checked every two weeks after half term. Meanwhile, new initiatives just kept on coming. The government was to pursue a payment by results strategy, which the unions said that they would fight. The local education authority announced that it would set up three education action zones in the county, of which our family of schools was to be one. That was in addition to special measures and the dismantling of the middle schools to consider.

I also had a naughty girl to deal with. I had sought help and advice from four senior staff and each one had, at one time or another, said *"We had better get her mum in"*, and walked off, leaving it at that. I had just an inkling that they were waiting for me to say *"Well, I'll get her mum in then, shall I?"* However, overall, and at that moment, I thought that things might have been settling down a bit. It did not seem to be quite so wild and anarchic as it had been.

In May, I saved a boy from a serious beating, when a nasty piece of work from another class came along with two intruders (older friends of his from outside) to administer some retribution for some reason that had not been explained to me. Once they had finally been ushered away, the intended victim got things out of his system by punching a hole in a window, having already purposely banged his head on the ceiling whilst standing on a desk in room two. You could not have made it up. When I had gone to help, the supply teacher said that he was coping OK with the people who were still in the room, but he needed someone to round up the ones who had walked out. Our intended victim returned, dripping blood all over the cloisters, to go with his, "It always happens to me", hang-dog expression.

The "would-be assassin" of room 2 later turned up in a GCSE exam that I was helping to invigilate, which he graciously attempted without his two minders being present. He was told by two members of staff to stop gouging holes in the desk he was sitting at. He was then asked to stay behind, but instead, he made a point of brushing past me on his way out as I purposely stood in his path. I suspect the school was being a bit cagey with this one. My bet was that his recent appearance with us was because he had been expelled from somewhere else and had come to us to finish year eleven and take some GCSEs. We were never told stuff like that. It was done on a "need to know" basis and probably in protection of his human rights, which apparently included vandalism and potentially (and only avoided by a whisker) serious assault.

We were expecting a few weeks of heavy attention ahead - planned visits from the humanities adviser and also a maths inspector looking at "maths across the curriculum," which meant that he had an excuse for turning up anywhere and at any time. Then it would be HMI again before the end of term.

The head of history was really unhappy about a proposal to bring in an open option system, thus doing away with the degree of protection that history and geography were both previously awarded. They were also considering the introduction of a general humanities qualification, which, though I had tried it before with some success (I thought, though I was not sure anyone else shared that view), would now further erode the take up for both of our more traditional disciplines.

By Mid-July, I had received 7 inspections in three weeks. The adviser pasted me over a poor showing with a year nine class, but I rescued it with a year ten one the next day. Then I had the local education authority maths man with year 12, which was OK, then the quiet one, who told me that my registration group held me in respect. I hoped that I had not look too surprised. The adviser came back to the same year nine session the following week. It was rubbish and I thought that I had finally been rumbled. I have never felt so down-hearted by the end of the day. What hurt most was knowing he was right. It was poor.

Mixed ability year nines with thirty in there. I just didn't enjoy it at all.

School was by that stage officially making reasonable progress, after the most recent visit from HMI. They would be back in October and again in March 2000.

Before the end of the summer term, I was summoned to the head with other heads of faculty and the year heads. Nine out of the twenty-four lessons observed by the HMI team were unsatisfactory and there were apparently some surprising names on the list. That was all designed to worry people. At least I went public about how rubbish this system was before people started thinking I was rubbish as well. Why was this such a rubbish system? Because it demeaned people, labelling them unfairly as failures in their chosen occupation, because it put undue pressure on people just because they happened to work in a particularly difficult situation at an especially difficult time, because it was draining the job of its fun and spontaneity through the perpetual burden of having to prove yourself all the time, and because nobody was interested in your contribution over decades of hard work and you were only as good as your most recently observed lesson. Your record over years could then suddenly count for nothing.

We were constantly on the receiving end of political posturing, whether it was Thatcher getting tough with teachers or Blair bleating on about public service intransigence in the face of necessary change. We were convenient pawns in a game of *"We are tougher on incompetence than you were"*. Yet, the profession was full of well-meaning people who just wanted to spend a career helping relatively disadvantaged young people to get on.

That was all we wanted to do - just help people. Why did they want to pillory us, blame us, name and shame us all the time? We were trying hard but instead of thanks, we only got more and more judgemental negativity. It was so stressful to be always on the receiving end of this propaganda. All the good humour had been squeezed out of the job.

A girl with a stud through her tongue said to me "*My sister said you used to be strict.*" I felt my legs buckle as though she had sliced them off at the knees. She had summed up my problems in a nutshell. I was no longer recognised as being fully in control. I was probably already seen by many as a soft touch. I had always thought that I was right in the middle, between the old hard liners I'd met both as a pupil and in my first school as a teacher, who I did not want to be like anyway, and those who struggled and might have done so anywhere. I wanted to be thought of as firm and fair and I believe that I was exactly that for most of my time. So, what happened? To survive through the dark days, I bent over backwards to try to avoid confrontation. I lost faith completely in those who were supposed to help us. I did not bother them. I lowered my standards. I chose to compromise. In some instances, I put up with things I had never previously allowed, like bits of swearing, pupils talking over me or graffiti on exercise book covers. The kids latched onto this. They thought that I was not interested in them enough to fight for what I believed in, and in the end they were right.

I could remember the exact lesson that I first turned off in my head - the room, the class, the desk I sat at, many of the faces, the time of day, the afternoon sunshine through the window. I thought I've had enough of this. I do not have the energy to fight any more. There was a bit of noise and I wanted to say something and I just thought, "Forget it. I can't be bothered". I had been a different teacher and a different person ever since and I knew I could never recapture it thereafter.

I continued to live off the reputation I had made for myself in earlier days. With upper sets and sixth formers, they probably would not have noticed the difference, but many of the others did. I could still teach and I could still get good results, but only where the kids wanted to work. With the rest I just gradually folded in the face of the battering I had received year after year from badly behaved and largely lower ability kids who were not the slightest bit interested in what I wanted to do with them and for them. I could no longer muster the energy to try to put it right. I was totally dismayed by the undermining lack of support we had had to endure from our managers since the beginning of the school in 1993. I think they were as much to blame as I was for the condition that I later found myself in.

Even "A" level was going wrong. Of my three candidates, one dropped out, one was kicked out and one failed. What a mess it was. I needed to find some resolve, not least before the adviser came back to see my year nine class. After that disaster, he had asked me why I had not been more forceful with a girl who had come in late and answered back when I questioned her attitude. He told me that he would have come down on her like a ton of bricks. I told him I'd tried that and it had ended up in a slanging match, in which she was actually screaming at me. She had been a pain for all sorts of people all year. When I had checked with the senior management team, who offered me no meaningful assistance, I found out she had twice been suspended from her middle school. What was I supposed to do? The inspector told me he thought I had lost my calm assertiveness. Thanks. I would have liked to see him handle that class. Now that would have been fun.

Our impact in lessons was affected not just by teaching strategies and classroom management techniques but by the attitude the kids brought with them to the class from the start. That could have been affected by the time of day (shorter attention spans in the afternoon), the lesson they had just come from (it could have been a complete circus), how well they had slept the previous night, how much and what food they had eaten for breakfast and lunch (too much sugar, etc), what they had got up to on the way to school, the general hardships they faced as a matter of course whilst out of school and even who they had (literally) bumped into on the corridor on the way to your class. Those things could all have affected the way that they behaved when they finally got there.

There was a good article in the Guardian by Peter Preston, who said that we have selection by neighbourhood these days. That seemed to be about right. He also added that "M*ixed ability teaching has been dubbed the creed of a slightly loony sect*". I thought about waving that one in front of the head.

I provided a bit of a rushed job on our department's exam review before going on the sixth form field course and the head passed it back to me as inadequate, as he had done with all the rest, apparently, apart from maths. We all had to rewrite them.

Thursday afternoon registration was lively. A boy and a girl in my class did not like each other. He sniped at her. She over-reacted. I advised them both. They ignored me. She started shrieking, picked up a chair and started hitting him across his back with it as he cowered. I got up and moved towards them and she turned and went to sit down. They started mouthing at each other again. She picked up the chair and hurled it across the room in his general direction. I jumped out of the way. I had been standing between them. I reported it to the head in a referral. The next day the girl was in, but the boy was not. There was no message from the head. It was as though it had not happened. I must get around to asking him about it, I thought.

The head called a meeting to ask the heads of faculty for their involvement in a system euphemistically described as "support for colleagues" that HMI had earmarked as in need of improvement. He read out a list of eight names. I was half expecting to hear mine. I stopped listening when he named my colleague and friend from both the current school and the previous one. Just one lesson had been failed, by one grade, by one inspector, on one occasion. Not exactly a total indictment, then, after many years of successful hard work and good order in the class room. I felt absolutely gutted. My belief was that this supposed "supportive intervention" was a smokescreen for "we want to get rid of you because your face, for one reason or another, does not fit with our ideas for the future". I thought that it was a less than subtle way of pushing people towards the door. The stated criticism was over the pace of a lesson. I saw this as subterfuge - a red herring and an excuse. Consistently successful exam results over a long period of time and at both examination levels told a completely different story. We were talking about a highly respected figure, who was renowned for competent classroom management.

A letter is then delivered explaining the situation with regard to intervention and support. How would that make you feel? A whole career thrown back in your face. I should have said to the head, "Stuff it". Here is the letter that I should have written to him.

"Dear Head Teacher,

Having thought more carefully about the role you outlined for me in the forthcoming Advisory and Inspection Service's support programme I realise I can't take part in it. For my friend and long-standing colleague to be identified as needing such support is one of the most monstrously unfair decisions I have ever come across. If I were the parent of a child who had just learnt that they were going to have this teacher for a two-year examination course in the following September, I would say, *"That's good, a safe pair of hands. My child will do as well as he or she is able to under this person's guidance"*. I know that this supposed corrective measure is all phoney. It is a charade and a pretext. You are likely to only need one full-time teacher in that area in the future and the other one is competent, younger and cheaper, so you are edging my friend towards the door. I think that you see my colleague as being "old school" and therefore not fitting in with your vision for the future. How can you believe that it is the right thing to do, to undermine people so totally, by trying to destroy their self-confidence when they have given excellent service over a significant period of time? It stinks and I want no part in it."

I sent a watered-down version to the head, certainly it was minus the last section. The head told me that he had been left with no choice, as these were Ofsted's own recommendations. Ofsted would notice if something wasn't OK and they would return for that thing the next time. I said that any balanced view would surely show my colleague winning on points by a mile and that we all had different qualities that we brought to bear. The head asked me to show the letter to my colleague, which I had intended to do anyway.

Of all the duties we had to do, bottom of the drive after school was the most testing. Hard-faced, baseball-hatted youths mooched around at the top of the drive. They should not even have been on the premises. Should I have told them that? No, thanks, it would have been to invite a volley of abuse. Stony-faced parents waiting for their children sat revving up their cars, partially blocking the foot of the drive and causing an obstruction on the main road. They then drove off too fast, impatiently threading their way through the crowds whilst kids were still trying to cross the road. Morose gangs of our kids, all out of uniform, but who should have been in school, waited for their mates, in the company of glowering past leavers who hadn't yet got a job. It was sometimes depressingly forbidding out there.

The French teacher went home after her "chat" with the head and the inspector. She would not be coming back. That left us with a varied bunch of multi-talented triers. Any remotely incompetent people had now left us.

I survived one diabolical year nine lesson and made it to the October half term holiday. I noted that I had bust a gut that term and that I had a clear conscience. By Christmas, HMI had come and gone again and the verdict was that we were making reasonable progress. The head was talking positively about the future. They were planning to build a new humanities block.

The former second deputy head under the previous regime had been to the head to complain about others that he said were side-lining him, presumably because of their perceptions of his past role with the previous management. That would have no doubt included me and my assistant teacher in the geography department. The head rightly took it up and interviewed me and two others and then asked me to make a written statement. A meeting was then arranged for January, when it was to be discussed. I couldn't fault the head on that one. He was trying to move on and there was a lot of resentment directed at the former members of the senior management team who had survived the cull. I actually played a pretty straight bat with the gentleman in question. I was aware of the danger and I did not want to give him any reason to have a go at me, so I thought that I would be OK over it.

By April 2000, we were out of special measures. In the pub to celebrate, the head asked me what I thought about it. I just said that I was relieved and added that I was opposed to the whole name and shame scenario and I left it at that. After all, we were officially no longer failing, officially no longer providing an unsatisfactory education for our charges, but what a total load of nonsense the whole wretched performance had been. Still, I expected that they wouldn't be back for two years, or so. There was never a dull moment. In that year, we had performance related pay to look forward to and the next year it was to be the reorganisation of the middle school system.

In June, we had a knees-up at a local restaurant to celebrate our success with regard to special measures. The self-congratulatory speeches were sickening. Earlier the same day, we were reprimanded for a failure of communication over the year twelve exam arrangements, which had been a mess.

I was pleasantly surprised to find out that I passed all my Ofsted inspections with the same score - 4 - Satisfactory. Internal restructuring would mean applying for my own job yet again. The structure for the new 11-18 school was published in October. There would be no faculties anymore (again), so I would have to apply for the head of geography post, one more time.

Someone mentioned in passing that we never got a pat on the back for minor successes. This was generally true, but actually I was commended in the exam review meeting for my "A" level results, which were probably the best I had ever had, with all eleven candidates passing.

In the previous year, I had been taken to task for the quality of my written departmental exam review. Consequently, I made sure that in the year that followed, it was top notch, but they postponed the meeting, then they forgot the re-arranged date and when it was finally to happen it was to be squeezed into a twenty-minute slot, then they postponed the evaluation part because the deputy was "*not around*", and I was left still waiting for it. Rigour was apparently something that applies to some but not necessarily to all.

I was actually "up to here" with accountability by then. We were told that we had to submit written plans for our use of in-service training time, presumably because we couldn't otherwise be trusted to work purposefully within our departments. Then we had to write an evaluation of what we had successfully managed to do in the time. I knew what to do and I knew how to do it. I just needed the time itself, without any extra form filling nonsense that blatantly reduced the time one had to do the business.

In January 2001, I completed the application for my own job for the fourth time in eight years. Discipline was slipping again. There was too much staff absence and there were too many supply teachers around once more. The new buzz word now was inclusivity. It meant, for our immediate purposes, that nobody was being excluded, so we were back into the old pressure cooker routine. I had lost it with one year ten class and nearly so with three very troublesome girls in the other one.

By March, I had my job again and I was to be subject manager for geography. I had also passed through the threshold for performance related pay. Perhaps I was not so bad after all. There was a staffing crisis nationally, we were told. It had always been a matter of supply and demand. They would never ever pay us more than they needed to in order to retain a teaching force of just below the sufficient total strength.

I discovered that I had high blood pressure. This is how I recorded it on the day, probably rather proving the point as I wrote it down.

"I thought I was fairly fit - I am not over-weight, I take regular exercise, I don't smoke. Could it be stress? Four enforced job application procedures in rapid succession just to keep my own job, two years of special measures, countless inspections and observations, standing in for the classes of a recently retired colleague, trying to catch up with the coursework he did not do before he left so that his class do not miss out, arriving at 7.30 for the last two years to write my lesson plans, dealing with a string of supply teachers on a daily basis since the only linguist in my faculty left at Christmas, responsibility for introducing GNVQ, which turned out to be a bit of a fiasco, the impact of the "inclusion policy" on class sizes and discipline, a new "A" level syllabus to prepare for, preparations for teaching 11 to 12 year olds for the first time in my life, meetings with the external verifier for GNVQ who was not overly impressed with my efforts in that direction so far, attending meetings of the numeracy group, attending meetings of the environment group, the completion of the European Driving License for Information and Communications Technology to deal with, performance management plans to submit, volunteer mentoring for two year eleven pupils prior to exams, volunteering for after school revision classes, a full timetable to teach, a department to run, a faculty to oversee over recent years (twice over), I have not missed a day through illness for two and a half years and there are only three lessons a week when I am not teaching/on call/supervising the quiet room.

I put up with incessant low-level bullying in my registration class. We have endured one serious assault, leading to one boy being moved out and other kids moved within the room. Yesterday one of my boys sprayed hairspray on a piece of paper in someone else's classroom, lit it with his lighter and then got it stuck behind a radiator and they had difficulty extinguishing it. I have to follow this up. Also, this week I had to step in between one boy and another one that he was attacking in my class. Last week I was the only member of staff around at break to stand between two girls about to start a fight and being encouraged to do so by a 50 plus crowd and I met with physical resistance as I tried to make my way through the inner ring of potential fight supporters who had literally closed ranks. I received sporadic verbal abuse whilst on drive duty. The smokers, having already lit up before they had left the premises, all have to be challenged. I repeatedly check the toilets on break duty which stink of urine and cigarette smoke and there is not even much respite in the staff room where kids throw the door open periodically and run away. How damaging is this repeated requirement to challenge relentless bad behaviour in our officially improving school? It is confrontational, however low-key you try to make your intervention. Aggression is endemic in our school's subculture. It is par for the course, day in, day out. No wonder I have high blood pressure!"

Amazingly, my next diary entry was a whole year later. I sorted out my medication eventually, which I would be on for the rest of my life. At least I would get a regular health check out of it. It did affect my confidence to tackle the miscreants. I know I should not have got worked up or taken it personally, but that was actually very difficult. You were only putting on an act up to a point. Essentially, it was still you that was doing all you needed to do. You couldn't divorce yourself from the processes to that extent. It would get to me. One of my coping strategies had been to have a couple of alcoholic drinks on most nights of the week. It became a habit, like an anaesthetic. Obviously, that was not good for high blood pressure, either. I started to think seriously about taking early retirement. I had never thought it would come to that. I had always thought in the past that I would breeze it to sixty and then do something else. The truth was that the strain of the previous ten years had probably caught up with me. It had been a hectic year, working on two sites for the first time and travelling backwards and forwards between them, thus taking time off any limited relaxation or preparation opportunities at break or lunchtime. My reward, however, was to be a brand-new humanities suite from September and a new classroom in the new block.

We faced yet another advisory service inspection and review. The inspector was in my room for 55 minutes and provided me with no personal feedback. I went to see the head about it on the last day of term. He said they had been unprofessional in not providing it. I had also been given the run around by my first ever year seven classes. Teachers who had been successful with them seemed to be treating them like infants. I tried to treat them like aspiring grown-ups and it back-fired completely.

Ofsted were due to return during the next year and I was beginning to think that I was past caring. This would be my 7th external inspection in eight years (1995 - county review, 1996 - Ofsted, 1997 - quality assurance review, 1998 - county review, 2000 - Ofsted, 2002 - county progress review).

My department appeared to be crumbling, personnel wise. 2000 - full-time assistant left after a probe into his departmental contribution, 2001 - totally inadequate replacement's contract was not renewed, 2002 - full-time newly qualified teacher resigned after one year, 2003 - my other part-time assistant announced her retirement.

By mid-April 2003, Ofsted had been and gone again. The department was "*satisfactory*". The school was "*good and improving*". Were they quite sure? I think they came with the announced intentions of distancing themselves from the mantra of the previous Chief Inspector for School, in an avowed attempt to be positive and look for good practice, as well as backing up what the HMI inspectors had only relatively recently concluded. I think the deciding factor now was probably ambience, which fitted in with the word on the corridors that they had made their minds up by the Tuesday of inspection week. Largely, this was - with one or two exceptions in year ten - because we had managed to get the kids onside, having effectively drawn a line under the previous regime. They had been persuaded to act the part. It was a propaganda success for the head's strategy in managing to build a bit of self-belief in them as well as in us. A few years before, with disaffection so widespread and resentment so apparent, it would not have been possible to cajole the kids into thinking that it was in their interests to put on a good show. That that became possible on the latest visit, even if it hid the everyday reality to a degree, was a small victory all round. It was the first time in the school's existence in its latest form that in spite of ongoing problems a feeling of togetherness had been created, even if it was based largely on a mirage. Nevertheless, many kids wanted to show that they were actually proud to be there. It was quite touching, really. After all, that was how it should be for everyone all the time.

My colleague, whom the new head had earlier seemed to have in his sights, was truly vindicated with a deserved *"very good"* from the inspector's observations. It just showed how ridiculously arbitrary the inspection regime could be and how vulnerable we all were to the snap judgements of passing inspectors, who could effectively pronounce on the curtailment of someone's career at the stroke of a pen.

One of the assistant geographers was taking a lot of time off, now that she had decided to leave at the end of the summer term. I had to deal with a succession of knackered old men arriving as supply teachers, who I was increasingly likening myself to.

Departmental results were poor that year. I had put up with a procession of supplies to replace my assistant, and the young teacher who moved on left her coursework in disarray, which I should perhaps have picked up and acted on more quickly. The man who was drafted into the department to help us out from another part of the school had, himself, also been off the premises for getting on for half the year.

One of our written GCSE papers coincided with a test taken by the whole of year seven, a massive collection of fidgeting little monkeys, inexplicably undertaken in the same hall at the same time, which someone must have mistakenly thought would be a good idea, in order to ease the pressure on staffing. It was a travesty, a constant barrage of interruptions from the younger kids, asking where to put their name and can they go to the toilet, that would have unsettled anyone trying to settle to a proper exam. It must have created totally the wrong atmosphere in the hall and been very costly in terms of marks not gained by the geographers.

I was thinking about not being there so much that it was starting to affect my performance. It got into my head and I almost unconsciously started to wind down. My year twelve class folded through lack of numbers, so I would have no new sixth form for the first time in 30 years. I offered to teach some sociology and tourism in the sixth form, instead. I was old enough to take early retirement. It was a relief to know that I could go when I wanted to. I planned to stay for another year if I could get a lot of sixth form teaching, geography or not. Everything depended on what my timetable was going to look like for the next year. If I kept going, I would maximise my pension, though I was actually less concerned about that at that moment. I was then thrown a lifeline by the departure of the person in charge of the vocational leisure courses. I swiftly asked the deputy head if geography could over-see them in future and she said yes. That meant that I would spend most of my teaching time in the sixth form, as tutor and teacher (potentially) of geography, sociology and leisure and tourism. I told her that I was taking it one year at a time from then on, depending on my likely timetable. The new regime had been pretty good to me, overall, I thought.

The head then said he was going. He would be working directly for the local authority as a member of the county's advisory and inspection service. I was not surprised. We would have another new head from September. The deputy, the present head's own appointee and a colleague of his from his previous school, was to take charge in the interim. Though generally well thought of, this was someone who had always been in his shadow, lacked his presence, was not visible enough around the place, and would have to appear to be more forceful, moving forward. I thought that the head had actually done a good job, overall, in difficult circumstances, but it was not a universally held view. Arguably, to be seen to have turned the school around and to have had that officially recognised by many people outside the school and maybe some within it, too, a cynic might have added, "Go now, because the only way from here is back down again".

We had the same catchment, similar kids from what was still very much a deprived area, massive curricular upheaval that had not yet had time to bed in, a reorganised school still operating on a building site, a school which would be under the inspectorate's microscope for years to come, continuing discipline problems that we were probably handling a bit better because we were more of a united team than we had been before and high rates of staff absence and legions of supply staff, as ever. Though positivity had replaced conflict and mutual distrust, the advances were tentative in many respects, built largely on staff goodwill and always in danger from further potential traumas in the community that we served. It was fair to pay tribute to the head, who would have been in the post for seven years, he reminded us, in his signing off letter. I had often thought, on watching him in action, that I would have done it like that had I been in his place. He never raised his voice, yet he held their attention. He was respectful to all he addressed, even on the odd occasion when they were not being respectful to him. Indeed, he never appeared to be flustered, even when faced with those who had completely lost the plot.

The other deputy he appointed from outside had also grown with the school over the few years up to that point and had now moved on to a headship elsewhere. He deserved it. He had grafted tirelessly and I had a lot of time for him. He was a committed and compassionate teacher, who had developed in stature during his time with us. I saw in both men the determination to do the right thing against all the odds. I liked to think that I once shared their focus and professionalism, to act with conviction to improve the lot of young working-class kids, often from troubled backgrounds. I did not share their drive and ambition to get to the top on a personal level, but I felt that I made my contribution all the same. They had both been straight in their dealings with me, for which I was grateful. At the same time, they both made me feel a bit inadequate. I saw in them what I might have been myself, if I had been braver and had possessed greater ambition.

I resigned on the 17th of January 2005. More accurately, I let the acting head know over lunchtime in the dining hall that I intend to take early retirement at the end of the academic year and she gave me her blessing. I felt relieved, but sad. My career was fizzling out through lack of energy. I could not have foreseen that ten, or even five, years before. I had run out of steam. I did not want to do nothing in the future. I would look for something else to do as soon as I finished in the summer. All I knew was that I did not want to do what I was doing anymore. I could not have been more certain of it. Yet, I also had big mood swings. After a good lesson I thought, what have I done? After a bad one, I thought, thank God I'm going.

When passing him around the place one day, the post-troubles head of sixth form told me that I was a good teacher and that what he liked about me, particularly, was that I was always fair to the kids, "*unlike some*", he added. I made a mental note to have another word with him. I didn't always take compliments graciously. I kind of brushed them off. I think it was embarrassment. I would tell him I was grateful for his kind thoughts.

The job description for my position was up for perusal and that created an air of finality about it. I asked the curriculum deputy about the possibility of any short-term part-time opportunities, but her body language said no before she had opened her mouth and I straight away regretted having made the enquiry. She was quite astute. She reminded me of the former head at the girls' school. She was clever and probably more ruthless than her friendly exterior suggested. I think I had upset her at an earlier Inset event when we were talking about schools making specific appointments for behaviour managers and I caustically said we used to call them deputy heads. People like her often now hated that part of their job. They were a bit of a new breed. Being a policewoman, sweeping up the naughty kids, being on call and being on duty around the place all took up to a whole day of her week, she had complained more recently. Well, fancy kids getting in the way of a well-run office job. It struck me like a flashback. At least they had their plush office bolt-holes to retreat to in order to get over the latest little conflict situation they had inadvertently come face to face with.

I finished on the 26th July 2005. The female appointee impressed at interview, I was told, though obviously it was nothing to do with me. I was not consulted and I did not get to meet her. That was how they like it in those circumstances, no embittered old fart around to put anybody off. Since February, school had just gone by without me. I was there in body but not in spirit. No one had talked to me about next year. For the first time, I had no planning to do. I just felt left out. People were kind but repeated the same things, time after time, "*You must be counting down the days*" and "*What will you do with your time?*".

Leaving, itself, was difficult. I had to make three speeches, one at an impromptu lunch arranged by the sixth form tutors (I spoke about reminiscences), one at a meal out in town in the evening during the last week of term (I spoke about valuing one another, because when you sever your ties, you realise how important those links have been) and after school on the last day at the presentation and goodbyes, where I think I spoke a little too cockily without meaning to, but maybe just about got away with it. People paid me some nice tributes. The head of the sixth form said I was someone he looked up to as a first-class example of a middle manager. The head of English, who had been given the job of saying an official goodbye, as he had known me a lot longer than the rest of the hierarchy, said I was a highly principled teacher. This was based on his memory of an incident when I walked out of a meeting with the first deputy head, after she had denigrated my colleagues and at a time that I thought that she herself was very much to blame. I had heard enough. I was actually only selectively highly-principled, however. My mind immediately shot back to a time at least fifteen years earlier. The head of special needs at the girls' school believed that I was going to take issue with her at a staff meeting that evening. I was conscious of the fact that we did not see quite eye to eye over the issue, whatever it was. Half way through the afternoon she stopped next to me in the staff room and passed me a Lion bar. "*It's for you*", she said and moved on. I ate it, just as the penny dropped. She was buying off my opposition with chocolate. At the staff meeting, I kept my mouth shut (that time, but too late). I have been reminded of my lack of resilience every time since then that I saw that particular confectionary on sale. I never ate another one again. Ever.

I found the most difficult thing was saying goodbye to the forty odd people I wanted to exchange a personal word with. It got worse with each one and I'd saved the trickiest ones until last. Some people seemed as sad as I was that I was going, which took me by surprise. I was given a very generous parting gift by my colleagues.

The authority sent me a questionnaire to complete, wanting to know why I had taken early retirement. I ticked the "pupil behaviour" and "stress" boxes. That covered it, and in the space at the bottom of the page, I explained the obvious link between the two.

There is no automatic way of gradually winding down towards the end of a teaching career. Theoretically, I could have carried on making useful contributions to upper school examination classes, but that's not how it works. My replacement deserved the opportunity to operate across the board and make their own mark, as I once had. When you have got to go, you have got to go!

6. Now, Let Me Get This Right

That was the end of the diary that I kept while I was in school. I went on to help young people with autism for a further six and a half years, firstly as a learner support and then as a tutor, before retiring from education completely after a career of over forty years.

I did not revisit my notes until 2013, the year after I had finally retired. By then, I had not looked at some of it for nearly two decades. When I started to write it, I had viewed it as a personal safety valve. It was only after I had drawn a line under my career that I thought about making an account that was accessible to others.

The usual scenario had been that I would drive home mulling over the events of the day, and if I had felt I had been under particular pressure, I would make straight for my desk and my diary and offload.

My diary also operated in fits and starts, sometimes offering information profusely and at other times leaving things unreported for weeks or even months. For large parts of my last decade in school, I just got on with things as happily as I could, so that I had no need for the agonising that characterised the more agitated sections. I was surprised to notice that I actually completed a whole school year, comparatively late on, without feeling the need to add a single entry.

That rawness to the times is now what strikes me most and the seemingly relentless pressure of the daily encounters. Yet, most of the kids were always good company and I loved the challenge of trying to edge them forward. I did not mean it to sound disparaging when describing them as "kids". That was how they were described by most teachers throughout the time that I was involved. It was just lazy shorthand for pupils.

I have also avoided mentioning anybody by name, using instead a description of their position within the school hierarchy or the other relevant agencies. I wanted to comment only on the way that people had responded in their particular roles. I made up names for one or two pupils where the narrative demanded it.

Although the story is true to the best of my knowledge, I'm sure that others will have seen things differently. Nor was I privy to everything that happened, so it is certainly not the whole truth either. I believed that we were poorly served by a number of colleagues, who really should have been more supportive. I was also pretty sure that this was extremely unlikely to have been the sole incident of its type. Comparable dramas must have played out in schools in similarly deprived areas and at roughly the same time. My guess was that many of the situations described here would be all too familiar to many former teachers who worked through the 1980s and 1990s in some tough urban settings.

I ultimately had faith in the fact that we live in a relatively healthy liberal democracy. It was a tale of how, in the end, with the help of a free press and with the determination of some well-meaning individuals, and eventually with the cooperation of the relevant agencies having belatedly been stirred into life sufficiently to exercise their responsibilities, a particular wrong was righted.

The years between 1997 and 2005 that followed our major upheavals were very different because the whole school staff was by then pulling in the same direction. The problems we faced had not gone away, though. They were deep-seated and reflected life in a very troubled community that was still going through the worst of times. Retrospectively, our school never really took off as a consistently successful entity all the time that I was there. The reasons for that were largely beyond our control to solve alone.

The social environment in which teachers operate remains very much a political issue to this day, in spite of the widely accepted mantra to the contrary - to try to keep politics out of education. How can you actually do that? For me, it was nonsense to imagine it that it was possible, or even desirable, at least for as long as real equality of educational opportunity remains a goal rather than a reality.

I liked to think that I approached the matter of helping my pupils to gain grades at the various examination levels in the same way that I would have done had it been me that was taking them. That was actually a far cry from my experiences during my own school days. I thought hard about how I could improve their chances, keenly trying to improve my own performance, year on year, turning things over in my head, time and time again, even while lying on the beach during the family's summer holiday.

The phone calls to the school office for "my" results on two consecutive Thursdays each August, from wherever the family happened to be - home or abroad - were real heart thumping moments for me and I treated good news as if I had just scored a hat trick in a cup final, punching the air on the walk back to the camp site, youth hostel or B. and B., from the telephone box in the middle of nowhere.

That was the critical bit for me - a series of slight, but hopefully meaningful improvements in the life chances of some steady, pleasant, well-meaning but generally under-confident, working-class kids. It meant everything to me as a teacher. I never really thought as much as perhaps I should have done about teaching children as individuals. I always concentrated on teaching whole examination level classes as one entity. I chased results for them all. Grades were paramount. Of course, I actually had better individual relationships with some kids than others, but I made a conscious effort never to individually put any of them on the spot or humiliate them or try to show them up for their lack of general knowledge. I always tried to improve their self-belief, bit by bit, by promoting a feeling of togetherness and common purpose.

I had tried hard to find relevance to the pupils' lives and backgrounds in the courses that I offered. I had become attracted to the concept of integrated humanities as a vehicle for capturing the attention of less academic kids, those who liked to tell me periodically that, "*Geography is boring, sir*". In my second school, I developed such a course, wrote about twenty topic information booklets and their accompanying tasks, resourced them, adopted them across a range of classes, marked the work and internally moderated it. It was a massive investment of time and effort for an experiment that, as it transpired, was only to last a few years. As a subject, it was eventually scrapped because it relied totally on coursework and such courses eventually fell foul of the government's efforts at increasing rigour, by tightening up on methods of assessment and especially those that were mostly assignments and not exam based. I acknowledged that there were weaknesses in the practicalities of running such a course, especially when the established external moderator, on whom I relied totally for validation, communication and support, proved to be just an additional problem to be overcome.

In 1992, she had fed back to me in her comments at the end of the cycle that there was *"Some undermarking, especially at the very top and bottom of the mark range"*. A year later and with the only thing that had changed in the meantime being the cohort of kids themselves and a slightly more generous interpretation of the mark scheme on my part, in line with her previous recommendations, she wrote in her feedback, *"Some assignments were rather generously marked, as they lacked the depth necessary to achieve the marks awarded by the centre"*. I thought about complaining to the chief moderator for the subject about the mixed messages and lack of consistency that I felt that I had received from the external moderator. It would not have done any good, I had concluded. The external moderator, in this instance, was also the chief moderator. I was stumped. I felt that she had made a mockery of the whole business and I had to admit that she had proved the government's point in the process. When the two schools amalgamated on the former boys' school site, the subject was subsequently dropped from the curriculum.

I had done all that work without a computer. I was slow to catch on to information and communications technology. I did not even do any typing. I wrote down everything by hand. When I needed to, I asked the school secretaries to type stuff up for me - though not my diary, which I had not shown to anyone at all, at any stage, and which still sat next to me on my desk at home, bulging in its original A4-sized, hard-backed, ring file. I carried on in more or less the same mode of very intermediate technology throughout my time at my final school. My computer and I would eventually become virtually inseparable but I was not the only one in my generation to have come through that transition the hard way.

I still believed, a whole teaching lifetime later, in comprehensive education. By that, I meant that I was not in favour of selection by ability at eleven years of age. I remembered from my own experiences how divisive that was for our own friendship group and for the wider society and what a massive impact it had on the discarded majority at the time of their rejection and in many cases, the mental scars it had left on certain individuals that I had known.

On the other hand, nor had I ever been in favour of mixed ability teaching at the secondary school level, which for a time did get a lot of support from practitioners and some commentators, but which was extraordinarily difficult to do justice to - for children aged thirteen anyway, and at the time and in the place that we were obliged to try it. The apparent gulf in intellect and certainly in attainment that had become the reality by that stage represented an enormous chasm of required differentiation that it was impossible to cater for adequately within a class of thirty young people. It might have sounded like a comforting egalitarian solution, but it just did not work. The amount of teacher preparation that would have been required for it to be viable was just not the best way to use that time, unless teacher/pupil contact time was going to be simultaneously halved.

My belief was that good comprehensive schools - and I knew that there were many - should be big enough, in terms of the sheer numbers of pupils on their books, to offer a real choice of subjects at fourteen plus and in their sixth-form, but they should also offer children of more limited ability, with a flair perhaps for one or two particular interests, the opportunities to develop within a system of setting that allowed all children to find their level across the board. That, I maintained, was what it was all about. Nobody should feel discarded and everyone should at least have the opportunity to shine at something. Even those who were likely to consistently occupy the lower ability sets or those who were in receipt of extra help just to cope, could then feel that they were also part of a successful school. They could maintain their family and friendship groups more easily across the ability spectrum because they were on the same site and they could take a full part in all the other activities that a healthy school had to offer them, which they could never have done in the past in the secondary modern school down the road, where they used to be shunted off to and where fewer resources were devoted to them when they got there.

It seems to me that what you end up calling schools and exactly how you fund them is less important. In fact, it sometimes just smacks of gimmickry. Whether they are community schools, specialist schools, academies, free schools, faith schools, or whatever, the essential issue is, firstly, that there should be access for all that is not based on ability and, secondly, that unless the right resources are going to be provided, one way or another they are still likely to fail.

I have felt that politicians have sometimes muddied the waters with these initiatives. They have claimed to widen parental choice of school type, but they have effectively chosen obfuscation. The impression may be one of encouraging greater diversity, but many parents will not have practical access to alternatives for their children. There is no real choice for those who are tied financially to where they live and for whom the local school, whatever it is like, is the only realistic option. They are denied any choice by logistical barriers. The real challenge is to make the nearest community school as good as those on offer elsewhere.

The polarisation that followed the insistence on measuring schools' performances increased the problems that already existed for schools like ours. Those parents with the facility to choose decided to send their children elsewhere, making ours not only a gradually smaller school but an increasingly poorer and weaker one, with a more skewed and bottom-heavy ability intake. This must have also happened in similar situations all over the country. However much the ministry and its agencies berated teachers in those institutions, which were still being named and shamed two decades later, the problems were largely of the government's own making. The stumbling block was a refusal to admit that such schools simply required the resources and extra assistance - in addition to sound internal organisation, effective management and a supportive staff - to enable them to do their job properly.

Most teachers in our failing school were first-class professionals. They brought their varied talents to the classroom though they were not necessarily recognised by those making judgements as first-class teachers in the measured sense. My experiences also reinforced the importance of having a good head teacher. The impact that a good leader can have on the success of the school and everyone in it can't be underestimated. Perhaps the biggest difficulty is hanging on to the good ones in the longer term.

I had an acquaintance who was a departmental head in a very successful comprehensive school with a distinctly middle-class catchment area, and who later worked for the local authority in an advisory capacity. He spelled out the difference between our two jobs. *"Your trouble comes from the kids, whilst ours comes from the expectations of their parents"*, he told me. He was almost right, except that at our school we got trouble from the parents as well, but it was of a different kind. While his school's parents sometimes placed unreasonable demands on him to favour their own children in one way or another, ours were often disinterested or uncooperative.

Although our parents' evenings theoretically provided the same opportunity to chase up problems with sons and daughters, I found that they were generally not well attended. If our staff saw half of the year group's representatives it would have been a very good night and attendance was often nearer to a quarter.

Meanwhile, at the comprehensive school that my wife and I were fortunate enough to send our own children to, parental attendance rates at such events were almost always approaching 100%. Down town, school tended to attract the parents of well-behaved kids, which was hardly surprising. The parents that we really wanted to see, because we needed their active cooperation, were rather more reluctant to put in an appearance and this often meant that additional phone calls or personal letters had to be sent home just beforehand as a prerequisite, even though this would not work either in some cases. A fair bit of cajoling was often necessary to bring them up the school drive at any time.

Once seated opposite to the teacher, it generally tended to be good news that I was relaying, but I remembered that on many occasions if I brought up a particular child's shortcoming, responses often fell in to one of two categories, either, "*You do what you like with him, sir*," or, "*Wait until I get him home*", neither of which were satisfactory answers, as far as I was concerned. They also frequently had their off-spring in tow, so that the youngsters were sometimes on the receiving end of a cumulative and humiliating ear-bashing, as they moved from table to table.

That some parents never wanted to set foot in school at all no doubt reflected their own unhappy experiences as young people in education a generation earlier. They still saw school as the enemy, along with all the other finger-wagging representatives of the state that they thought were against them, like the police, social workers, the Department of Health and Social Security and the educational welfare officers. What chance did we have with their children, in the face of such alienation? When such parents had to be specifically summoned to school, to help unravel some fairly major misdemeanours, even then they would try to send grandma or simply prevaricate. They often blamed school, anyway, for either being *"too soft with him"* or being *"on his back all the time"*.

I once made a big mistake on break time duty when patrolling an "out of bounds to pupils" area, where smokers might have been lurking. As I approached a corner of the building, I just caught sight of a man who was perhaps in his early thirties simultaneously disappearing round the next corner and obviously looking a bit lost. Instead of following him until I was in full view and introducing myself to him as I should have done, or simply calling out with a friendly, *"Hello!"*, I whistled. The guy spun back around the corner and without coming any closer to me, pointed forcefully at me and yelled, *"Don't you ever whistle at me again!"* He was livid. It had been a mellow, muted, enquiring, unaggressive, abbreviated, rising note sort of whistle, which I had thought, momentarily, was actually a fairly non-confrontational way of simply attracting the bloke's attention, as I was not sure up to that point if the man had even seen me. Assuming that he was a parent - though I would never know that for a fact, I had simply wanted to offer him some advice about the directions to the office, that he was clearly having difficulty in finding. I muttered an apology and continued straight into my helpful directions. The gentleman in question strode past me with a glare, and without another word vacated the premises. Today, intruders would be routinely challenged as a matter of course. The assumption that I made on the spur of the moment, at that time, and well before the sea change in attitude to making schools the generally safer environments that they are today, was that the guy probably had a legitimate reason for being there but lacked the social skills to go with it. Of course, it was a bit rude and thoughtless of me and I regretted it immediately. I admitted to myself that the bloke had a point that it was not the most appropriate way to attract someone's attention - but talk about over-the-top responses! I just felt that some of these people were like coiled springs, always on the defensive, always on the look-out for someone who was going to do them down. They just oozed low self-esteem. You could see them glowering their way around the town. Their basic unhappiness with their lot in life was simmering just under the surface all the time, and they seemed to be just waiting for some unsuspecting person to take out their grievances on.

Even on the journey to work through the town, one was in danger of upsetting them. I had to share the road with them. It seemed like they were on tenterhooks, waiting for the slightest bit of bad driving on your part, that they could then interpret as you being disrespectful to them, so that they could then beep their horn at you, or glower at you or shout obscenities, depending on the severity of your "offence", as they were so keen to see it.

What a sad dump this is, I thought, as I drove home one day, having changed lanes in front of a motor cyclist, with a young lady as his pillion passenger. Presumably he had been about to make the same manoeuvre himself, so I had inadvertently blocked his attempt to overtake me on the inside, in the approach to the next set of traffic lights. You would have thought that I had tried to run them off the road. Having overtaken me on the outside instead and in the normal way, the couple both sat at the red light and stared back at me, mouthing insults, and not just there but for the next couple of miles up the hill out of town, as they continually buzzed around my car. It was very intimidating. It made me feel sick.

"My dad says I've got to stand up for myself". "My mum says if anyone hits me, I've got to hit them back". "My dad says don't take nothing from nobody". It is no wonder, I thought, that in the face of this intolerant, overly pro-active and prevalent "act now, think later" view of the world, that we continued to have problems with belligerence in school.

Occasionally, I would have an initially perplexing problem with a single girl. These were relatively few and far between, but a pattern became recognisable in the end. They were not in a group who were simply "having a go" at me for a bit of entertainment. They could be sullen and uncooperative in my presence - moody and irritable - and I eventually got the feeling it was because I was a man and it was not quite as personal as it had first appeared. I realised after a few enquiries that it was either known or suspected that these were girls who were on the receiving end of abuse at the hands of a man elsewhere, or else they were witnessing it close-up at home when it was dished out to their mum. The dislike that they clearly had for me was consequently because they "knew what men were like" and they were presumably tarring them all with the same brush. These girls would either scowl at me or appear strangely vacant, and their behaviour in the classroom was often unpredictable. One of them cut her wrist badly on the glass panel that she had suddenly punched a hole in when passing, with nothing immediately evident to precipitate her action, except of course, the very real hurt she carried around with her all of the time.

Sometimes, glimpses of family life came spilling out into the room, regardless of who was in there. *"If my dad hits my mum one more time, I'm going to kill him"*, shouted one girl, as she swept into the room one day, having noticed that her friend was already sitting there waiting for her at a desk at the back. She was totally oblivious to my presence as I stood there waiting to start the lesson. She was clearly exasperated and very emotional and she sounded like she meant it. I passed the information on and provided the context to senior staff, but it did not stop her making a thorough nuisance of herself for me throughout the whole of the rest of the year.

Such issues could easily have been encountered anywhere, of course, but it certainly seemed that family problems like this were magnified in areas where poverty was already rife, presumably due to the greater stress that people were constantly under in their daily lives whilst just trying to make ends meet.

When I had to deal with the energy question as part of the curriculum for advanced level geography in 1984 in the company of a girl whose boyfriend was a striking miner and another whose father had defied the strike call, you could have cut the atmosphere with a knife. Though I relished these opportunities to bring my subject to life, this was not just an academic argument for those involved. It was their livelihoods that were at stake.

I sometimes imagined how different my career might have been in a leafier suburb. I always thought that if I had taught in a comfortable school with a largely middle-class catchment area, I could easily have seen it through until the normal retirement age. As it happened, I did eventually go on to work in a less stressful educational environment from the age of 56 until I was 63, when my doctor finally asked me, *"How many teachers of your age do you know?"* to which I had to reply, "None". It must be time to leave and do something else, then, I had concluded. The realisation that I had hit the buffers in mainstream, however, had come over me quite quickly. Admittedly, it was some time after I had lowered the overall quality of my performance.

I had always loved the camaraderie of the communal staff areas. *"Teachers are nice people"*, a colleague from my first school had once emphatically informed me. That gentleman had enjoyed the company of people in other walks of life previously, including the army, which I thought was likely to have been the experience that had prompted his observation. I never had reason to argue with his assessment. The staff room was a great place to be, even during the darkest of times. I loved being a teacher - for the first two decades, plus, anyway, and I enjoyed the company of my colleagues immeasurably, throughout my time at work.

What had become a stimulating and exhilarating experience at times, and one which consumed most of my waking hours, eventually became just a job, from which I desperately needed to escape by the end of each term. The day-to-day demands wore me out in the end. I made the right decision for myself and that was to go early. In doing so, I rescued my health and saved a substantial amount of money that I would otherwise have spent on alcohol.

Retrospective snapshots of past events encapsulate how bad it got for me when I was in my last year at school and my intentions had become known to others, though not to the kids at that stage. The decision I had already taken soon affected the way that I was performing as I already had one eye on the door. In the short term, however, there were still pressing issues to deal with. It transpired that one particular door periodically loomed into view for the last few months of my time there - and for some time after I had left it could still bring me out into a cold sweat just thinking of it.

There was another troublesome family that we were catering for. Teachers sometimes sense that there is a major problem and they then suspect that in all likelihood a lot of people are actually working very hard behind the scenes just to keep the family together. Under these circumstances, it can actually be the lack of hard information coming the way of the teaching staff that sets alarm bells ringing. At the same time, we heard about incidents from all over the school relating to other members of the same family but particularly this boy in year seven, who was obviously, therefore, no more than eleven years old when I first met him. I did not teach year seven until the very last years of my career. I was unused to children as young as this and often turning up with reading ages much younger still, not to mention their lack of emotional development.

When things relating to families in trouble got really bad, those in the know tended to close ranks. The fact that as a mere classroom teacher it might have benefited one to be aware of what was going on behind the scenes was not a priority for the other parties concerned. Information was purposely kept secret on the "only those who need to know" principle, which operated under such circumstances.

I knew all about the blue files under lock and key in the office. The bulging thickness of some of those files bore testament to many an unhappy childhood. Happy and well-behaved children's files were wafer thin. Naughty boys' files were stuffed and dog-eared, or had already spread to occupy two blue card envelopes by the time they were half way through "big school". Perhaps, I thought, I should have spent more time with the files and in a perfect world I would no doubt have done so, but the truth was that I rarely had time to peruse them for long, nor were subject teachers ever encouraged to do so, even where they had the little colour-coded extra stars on the covers that indicated further and previously undivulged horrors within. It was not my inclination to deal with whole groups rather than individuals that made me steer clear of the blue files. I accepted that with easier access allowing further examination, I might well have discovered all sorts of extra dimensions to the young peoples' lives that I had not known about previously. These filing cabinets were kept locked up in an annexe to the general office, which was also itself often locked and where there was no facility offered to encourage teachers to sit down and read - no space, no chairs, no privacy and always the chance of an interruption.

At the back of my mind, however, I knew that this knowledge was unlikely to give me any practical solutions at all. The pupils' inclination - perhaps in many cases as a direct response to the problems they faced - was still going to be to make nuisances of themselves rather than get on with their work in the classroom, however well fore-armed and knowledgeable I might have become about the details of the dysfunction in their home lives that was contributing to their distress.

Possibly the only thing that I remembered from my days studying educational theory at college came from a session on philosophy and more specifically on the notion of "respect for persons". It was very straightforward, of course, and effectively conveyed the idea that you should treat other people as you would wish to be treated yourself. It was a flawless maxim, it seemed to me, and it struck a note at the time and I hoped that it had guided my actions as a teacher throughout my time in the profession. I liked to think that I had always been respectful to my pupils and that I had shown them the same sort of courtesy that I expected (but by no means always received) from them. In the heat of the moment, events no doubt eroded my tolerance levels somewhat, and I could not guarantee, retrospectively, that I had adhered to the principle at all times. It remained, nevertheless, a good guide to life. I hoped that I had shown this particularly difficult boy that I had in mind some respect, too. Deep down, I knew that there were reasons for the lad's actions that were nothing to do with me.

In any event, the situation had arisen when l had to reprimand this boy, who was a younger brother of two girls whom I had also taught without particular consequence. I couldn't remember the details of the lad's poor behaviour, though I can still, to this day, remember his face. He was probably being as awkward as he could be, interrupting, shouting out, producing no work and so on. He ignored all my instructions and so I told him to get outside the room and eventually he went. I was not supposed to do this, because he was then officially unsupervised. Paperwork in the form of the staff handbook informed me that I should, at that moment, seek help from my departmental head. This would not work either because I was the departmental head and the assumption was that because I had reached that exalted position, I would not be requiring that sort of help.

The next step would be that I was required to carry on enduring this boy's misconduct whilst at the same time sending a dependable pupil to the office with a note requesting help from the senior member of staff who was on call for this purpose. My classroom was miles (it sometimes seemed) from the office so that was going to have a bearing on developments from the off. Another of the problems with that system was that the on-call duty person frequently did not choose to come quickly enough to be useful and in fact there was no guarantee that they would come at all before the end of the lesson, and I needed help at that very moment.

The boy now started to interrupt the lesson from outside by firstly clipping the foot of the door with his shoe then by repeatedly opening it a bit then closing it again. The kids thought that this was hilarious and so any momentum I had regained since his exit had already been lost. There were clear guidelines issued to staff about physical intervention with children. We were only allowed to intervene bodily with children when there was a serious likelihood of self-harm or when they were actually attacking other pupils or staff.

"You can't touch me" and *"I know my rights"*, were directed at us with increasing regularity during my later years. I turned my attention to the boy again and told him not to touch the door at all. He ignored me again and reached up to the top of the door and started swinging on it, backwards and forwards, with his body now back inside the room and his arms wrapped round the top outer edge of the door. The lesson had completely degenerated and I felt totally helpless to act. My chest tightened and I slumped into my chair and just watched the lad swinging on the door. He carried on in total defiance of my instructions. I felt completely disempowered and alone. The on-call person eventually arrived and the boy was taken away. Nothing happened to him that I was informed of and although not a reliable attender thereafter, he still kept on coming back to my lessons, more often than not, for the rest of the school year. The perception from the class was that he had won and any respect they had left for me had taken an irredeemable nose dive. On the day, I had felt absolutely dejected and humiliated. I wondered how it had come to this. I went over it time and again in my head to see if I could have approached things differently. Perhaps I should have asked for the help of a colleague who was closer to hand at the outbreak of the event, but they would have been teaching. I had always hated the idea of that kind of interruption myself, when I was supposed to be the one offering assistance.

In the end, I was just too proud to ask. Afterwards, I made representations to senior staff and I gleaned sufficient information to understand - though I was never officially told the whole story - about the problems in the family and basically how the school was going to have to hold on to them all, even though the boy had probably done enough to warrant exclusion a number of times over already.

Sometimes, though not necessarily in this particular case, dad or mum was reportedly already in, or likely to be going to, prison and people were working flat out behind the scenes to stop the children having to be taken into care as a result of the loss of the bread winner, however that bread had been "won". That was how it was. They were our kids and so it was our problem to deal with. Exclusions were frowned upon and indeed measured as an indicator of the overall health of the school. The school could not attract attention to itself all the time by failing publicly to hang on to its naughty children. Therefore, it provided the staff with the old pressure cooker situation once again.

I was still bemused. I had failed to deal properly with an eleven-year-old who had point blank refused to do what I'd reasonably asked him to do, and who had disrupted my lessons time after time and refused to come to detentions I'd set for him, and he had his parents' backing for not turning up for punishments, anyway, and yet I had to keep on having him there doing pretty much what he wanted to. It just about finished me off. I could hardly believe that I was the same person who could oversee two hundred pupils through a regimented dinner time, with all its potential for chaos, yet day after day managed it perfectly well without event or trauma and often on my own. I had to pinch myself to remember that I had insisted on good behaviour and a quiet working environment for about twenty-five years, or so, and that I had frequently and confidently announced to all comers that this was *"not going to be a mess about lesson"*.

I was struck by an observation from the Chief Inspector of Schools, in response to the news that 40% of new teachers leave after five years in the job, because of poor discipline. I knew that that fitted in with my own recollections, especially later on in my career. The Ofsted chief blamed their lack of appropriate training and the unions. Well, he would, wouldn't he? He was barking up the wrong tree, but as an establishment figure himself, who else could he blame? After all, he had to find someone to blame because blaming was the name of the game these days and he was not going to go for the government, the kids or their parents who were perhaps more directly the cause of the young teachers' angst.

When I started out, I knew within days that I had messed up quite a bit by trying to be too friendly to the pupils. It took a year, perhaps, before I felt that I was in charge in a way that I felt comfortable with. By then, I was confident that I could have taught anywhere. I was proud that I had been able to maintain my own discipline for the next couple of decades at a level that I wanted to in all of the three schools that I had ended up in. It was actually built pretty much totally on self-belief and self-confidence. I acquired the confidence that I needed so that I felt that I could handle any situation with a combination of body language, an assertive demeanour and an appropriate choice of words. I knew that I no longer had to rely on outside help, except in the most extreme of circumstances. I learnt it by doing it and not by being taught it.

The incident with the door-swinging boy had been very much at the end of things, but I could remember vividly the very moment, some time before that, when I had mentally thrown in the towel. I can still picture the situation. I can see the faces in front of me and many are still recognisable. I know the particular classroom and hear the noise the door made when it closed. It was a Thursday afternoon in the summer term, but it was a cool day. It was a year ten class of thirty kids doing GCSE geography, but with no great appetite for learning. They were a set of middle-ability students who were generally amiable enough but without much of a noticeable spark about them, I thought - even though it was my job to inject the spark, not theirs. They were not a particularly troublesome lot. Everyone knew where they stood. The kids did not try it on much and it was normally quite plain sailing. Looking back, I knew that I could have worked harder for them, but a weariness was just beginning to set in, which I had not started to come to terms with. It was the first sign of drift.

I sat and wondered how I was going to respond to a sudden excited undercurrent of off-task babble. Unfortunately, it occurred at exactly the instant when I chose to give up in my head. I just sat there and pretended it was at a reasonable level that it was within my powers to put a stop to if I had wanted to, at any moment. I knew, and soon they knew, that something was different. I would not have let that pass in the session prior to that one.

I actually stuck around for some time after that, resting on my laurels, as it were, and using up the remnants of the goodwill and the reputation that I had previously established. In the end, I was left totally incapable over the door incident, as I withdrew and froze in the moment. I could not process what I had to do with that boy. I realised later that the seeds had been sown on that otherwise very ordinary Thursday afternoon. I knew what I should have said and done then but I couldn't bring myself to do it. The self-belief that I had built up and employed for decades had started to evaporate. I knew then that I had to go and I went on to plan my exit. I had lost my determination to fight to stay on top. I did not have sufficient energy left to maintain the standards that I knew had served me so well up to that point. It was also partly due to the extraordinary circumstances in the school up to that time. I knew that I had been worn down by the endless demands to be up for it, day after day, lesson after lesson.

7. Bumping Along at the Bottom

So, what of the school I left behind? Anecdotally, I knew that it had carried on towards the bottom of things and most notably the league tables. It succumbed to special measures more than once after I left. On one of those subsequent occasions, the Ofsted report condemning it said that poor achievement was largely due to poor behaviour. Well, there's a surprise.

I checked it out later on Ofsted's own website. The academy that opened on our old site in 2012 failed an inspection in 2013 and again in 2015, after which it closed in 2016. It opened again in the same year with the same name but as part of a different academy group. It was judged to be requiring improvement at the most recent inspection that I looked at, during 2019. It had half the children on the roll than it did in our time. They should certainly have been able to spread themselves out a bit. That might have contributed to an acknowledgement that behaviour was noticeably better than in previous reports. If that was true and became sustainable, then it would be a real advance. The miniscule sixth form was apparently being catered for at another site, so presumably they were bussed out and back in as an entity. I could not find details on the Ofsted website about the historic inspections that I knew something about. Perhaps that was part of a grand plan to escape from the indictments of the past by encouraging such information to fade in the memory and not tarnish the potential for the future with regurgitated stories of former woes.

Once your school was identified as failing by Ofsted, it was expected that they were unlikely to leave you alone until they were satisfied that substantial changes had led to long lasting improvement. That was, in itself, still quite an expectation, where the social situation in which the school existed remained unchanged. That meant that the problems it encountered just kept on coming at a rate not necessarily being faced elsewhere. Is that how it should be in the drive for higher standards? Is it fair to subject staff to much more frequent inspections just because of where they end up teaching? How many times do you have to watch someone teach before you can say, yes, they are OK, and then just back off a bit? The level of scrutiny that teachers in some areas have to get used to is enormously draining, yet they are likely to have proved time and time again that they are good teachers. They still have to keep jumping through the same hoop.

The career of one of my former colleagues had seemed to be on a knife's edge for a time towards the end of an otherwise impeccable career, until they came back and decided that the school still had a "very good" teacher, after all, something that we were already well aware of.

In mainstream secondary schools, struggling teachers would already have been shown up by a measurable decline in their exam results, compared both to their own earlier successes and also to the outcomes from other staff teaching the same kids. If senior staff had their welfare at heart, they would have already called them in to see if they could identify what was going wrong. Pastoral care might have become an important theme in schools as far as children are concerned, but mechanisms for looking after the well-being of staff had not changed at all by the time that I had departed from the scene.

The framework of educational provision has changed dramatically and become much more fluid than when the local authorities had control of the process. Free schools were set up as a new type of academy school, in 2010. They gave parents, teachers, charities and businesses opportunities to set up their own schools in competition with pre-existing local schools, regardless of any recognised shortages in the availability of pupil places in the area. Free schools, in common with independent schools and other academies, could employ teachers who do not possess the standard qualified teacher status. Since 2015, all new academy schools were to be regarded as free schools. Some commentators have claimed that having a free school in the area somehow boosted performance in nearby rival schools. Critics say they are a waste of money, creating school places in areas which don't require them and therefore endangering established schools with their very presence, a situation that quite appeals to those who believe that market forces should determine educational provision in the same way as competitive free enterprise businesses operate in industry. The strong survive and the weak go to the wall. It is difficult to see how a lot of opening and closing of schools can offer the stability required to nurture gradual improvement.

Prior to free schools, we had academies, and the school I left behind became one. Set up by the Labour government in 2000 and state funded directly from the Department of Education, rather than by the local education authorities, they were described as self-governing, nonprofit, charitable trusts. They do not have to follow the National Curriculum but they are inspected by Ofsted. They were intended to improve pupil performance and break the cycle of low expectation as it affected schools in run-down areas with a history of poor examination results. Reviews since have been mixed. The main criticisms appear to be that not enough rigorous assessment of the first cohort of such schools was undertaken before the scheme was expanded, and in 2016 the Educational Policy Institute cast doubts on any meaningful improvements in such schools when compared to council run schools.

Another local school that I have some knowledge of anecdotally is the lead institution in an academy trust. Again, following free market thinking, there is a supposition that good practice in this school can readily be spread - according to the principles of the trickle-down theory - to the less well performing institutions in the same trust. To this end, some senior staff (who were presumably promoted because they were good classroom practitioners, themselves) no longer teach as much as they previously did, but have responsibility for spreading the word to their colleagues in the other schools. The assumption is that they can tell them how to do a better job. This could sometimes be a flawed notion. Teachers want to do things their own way. They can be open to new ideas, but the expectation that they are going to take on board, wholesale, the methods and approaches of someone who has been sent along to tell them how to teach properly could lead to resentment and therefore backfire.

In my experience, the best way to improve your practice as a teacher of examination level classes is to attend regular exam feedback meetings with colleagues from other schools who follow the same exam syllabus. They are set up by the examination boards after each exam cycle. They were invaluable to me. You are not being preached at and you can adopt or ignore recommendations as you see fit and in line with your own requirements and inclination. That is true professional development at work. What works for someone else may or may not work for you. As a professional, you can make that judgement without obligation. Inferior exam results in the other schools that make up an academy group will not be because the teachers there are not good teachers. There are other factors at work.

For most of my career, the traditional way of paying teachers was by topping up a basic salary with yearly increments, thus rewarding seniority on the assumption that the experience gained made them gradually more proficient. During my last few years in school and starting in 2001, the government thought it a good idea to make us jump through some additional hoops for any increases in pay (and kudos) thereafter. It was called performance related pay and it has become an intrinsic part of the way that teachers have been rewarded ever since. In principle, I don't think that many of us at that time had any particular grievance about the proposal, in spite of the fact that it just created something else for us to deal with. As habitual improvers, we probably decided that we could adapt innovations we were planning to make to the required format, anyway, and it may even have helped us to get more focused over them, though I understand that the system is now much more refined and targeted than it was in its infancy. I had been self-motivated in relation to improving my performance from the moment that I started teaching. I passed the required threshold assessment, though because I was already at the top of my pay scale, I was not rewarded any further for doing so.

Since that time, other initiatives have been introduced to try to raise the standards of teaching in the classroom by providing financial incentives aimed at luring good graduates into the profession in the first place, keeping good teachers in the classroom rather than losing them to management roles, and using their expertise to coach other colleagues. Advanced skills teachers lasted from 1998 until 2013, excellent teachers from 2006 to 2013, and master teacher standard was then floated as the next big idea by both main political parties from 2014. It seems to me that they all potentially create divisions between school staff members that could lead to resentment. Performance related pay already raised questions of favouritism, because decisions for progression ultimately rested internally with headteachers. It strikes me that they are all part of the same mindset: - that only money can incentivise teachers, that teachers can't be trusted to do their jobs properly when left to their own devices, and that we must have more and more measurable accountability where tax-payers' money is concerned. It is back to the market place. The fact that the initiatives continue to come and go so frequently suggests that they haven't worked as well as was intended.

Differentiation of outcomes in education is largely about concentrations of poverty. It is closely related to national and regional economic progress - but felt so much more acutely at those particular, geographically specific, local levels - in the depressed urban areas where many of the most vulnerable members of society are concentrated, where deprivation is commonplace and hopelessness has often, sadly, become the norm.

The gimlet-eyed, "Lion bar" special needs lady at my previous school was an astute, experienced teacher. In her role, she would have been one of the very few members of staff to have regular opportunities to witness the pupils in their home environment at that time, in the early 1980s. From time to time, she would address certain of her colleagues very directly (and from very close quarters) and inform them that *"You have no idea what some of these children's homes are like"*. She delivered it with a chilling stare and the emphasis of someone who was not going to be taken to task over the observation. She spoke from her first-hand encounters. The kids I taught who inhabited these poorer areas used to argue vehemently with each other about the individual streets that they lived in, to prove a point that they were not right at the bottom of the pile. It was so depressing to listen to.

I recalled some of the hundreds of decent parents that I had spoken to at countless parents' evenings, who were desperately trying to bring up their kids properly under such difficult conditions in their own neighbourhood; just well-meaning and hard-working folk, surrounded by an awful environment in which to rear their children. It must have been such a tricky task from a variety of perspectives.

The task for society and its decision makers is massive and yet continued failure to solve the school problem in isolation of the wider societal problems is met with castigation and blame for its teachers, instead of the necessary increased understanding and support. It is only the eventual greater allocation of the necessary resources that can make the difference.

So, fundamentally, it seemed that nothing much had changed over the last two decades for this school, in spite of the fact that inspectors had come and gone, pronounced, imposed special measures, come again to check that progress was being made, noted some improvements along the lines they were looking for but acknowledging that more needed to be done, gone away again, only to return a year or two later to witness the same core issues preventing learning taking place at a universally acceptable level once more, regardless of the repeated clearing-out of some formerly key staff and the bringing in of their replacements.

Ofsted people have an agenda and they speak on behalf of the government and tow the official line, but their outbursts are often misdirected and their interpretations do not always attempt to address the truth of the matter. They refuse to accept that it is a problem that the school can't necessarily solve by itself. Their parameters are too narrow. Not only that, but they are also fallible, because it is just people judging other people and there are a multitude of factors affecting that decision, however objective they try to be.

We thought that we had witnessed an Ofsted team having the wool pulled over their eyes by the incumbent management in our school. When, soon afterwards, an accident of history propelled the school onto the national stage and into the full glare of publicity, HMI came back and overturned their own recent judgement. They had cocked up the first time, though they never admitted as much. If they can cock up once, they can do it again. I would guess that they approach schools expecting to find evidence that confirms the view they have already begun to hatch at a distance, going on its recent history and its measured progress, as exemplified by league tables, etc. These people are only human. Perfect impartiality at all times would require a super-human detachment.

I knew that in all the incarnations of the systems of judgement that I had witnessed in practice, there were critical points in the numerical scores that could represent a chasm of difference for the recipient teacher, depending on which side of a very thin dividing line you eventually decided to make your choice. It used to be between grades four and five in a seven-point scheme. Then it was between three and four in a four-point scheme and later they moved the goal posts again for it to become between two and three in a four-point set-up, where a four was simply "Inadequate". That is because three, "Satisfactory" was no longer deemed to be good enough. The former "Satisfactory" was now something that Ofsted believed was no longer just that. It now represented a situation which required improvement, which provided a justification, after Ofsted had left, or indeed, as the direct result of internal observations by the institution's own managers, to put both specific areas of the school and particular teachers through a corrective programme, so that they could move towards being "Good" in future. This is just all semantics. It is playing with words to provide a justification for getting after people. None of it is going to help address the root of the problems that well-meaning teachers face in the classrooms in deprived areas of the country.

Except that the two/three border line became a real and additional divide between being OK and not being OK. The law of averages suggests that although such judgements have to fall either side of a watershed, no way can they all be clear cut decisions. If you are looking for evidence that a school is not performing, because results you have seen suggest that that is so, then which way are those individual judgements in the classrooms going to go? If you are expecting to see that the school is gradually improving since you last went there and gave it a good seeing to, during which time they have been putting your recommendations for advancement into practice and results have started to pick up, however minimally, which side will you come down on then when you are in the classroom?

As I flicked through the cuttings that had attracted my attention during the intervening years since I finished teaching, I noticed a common recurring theme being recorded all over the country. Poor behaviour in the classroom was still having a massively detrimental effect on learning. Teachers were being blamed for it and that was leading to ongoing problems in retaining and recruiting staff. It felt like things hadn't moved on at all.

Enormous sums were being spent on training yet the profession was then haemorrhaging so much of that expertise as young graduates became fairly quickly disillusioned with what they found out was their lot. They also cited a lack of a work/life balance and the relentless imposition of new targets.

How sad and what an immense waste of resources that so many resourceful young people are leaving, feeling disillusioned in this way. Instead of blaming their training,

I thought that Ofsted should talk to the teachers themselves and find out first-hand what they think is going wrong with the culture that Ofsted themselves have helped to create. Not all those who contributed articles to the press were in 'difficult' schools, nor were they all blaming the kids or their parents for their discontent.

I don't think that Ofsted should be scrapped. I believe that there is a place for a body that oversees the performance of schools and that it should be truly independent. Greater cognisance should be given to the socio-economic background of the school and I would like them to take note more sympathetically of the school's previous inspection history. Why do they assume that there is no difference in the milieu in which teachers operate in different places that just might have an impact on their overall effectiveness, when almost every experienced teacher knows that the opposite is true? I want to see more compassion, understanding and support for teachers in areas which face significantly greater challenges. I think that the inspectorate should be able to make positive and helpful suggestions based on the assumption that they will have gleaned enormous amounts of data about good practice elsewhere, and not simply say *"Get it sorted because we'll be back to check"* and then leave it to a new team to be even more rigorous in weeding out bad practice than the last lot, but in reality, changing nothing of substance and contributing to further failure down the line. Instead, they need more - and more varied - resources. In short, they need more money to be spent on them.

I stopped taking such a close interest in educational reforms and initiatives around 2016. Perhaps, Mrs May's retrograde grammar school plans were the last straw, though I prefer to think it was more positive involvement in other projects of my own that caused me to drift away. I satisfied myself that whatever the latest moves from above were going to be, it was really just more of the same as far as teachers were concerned, adding up to a continuous move towards proscribing how things ought to be done in the classroom and leaving less scope for individual decision making as a trusted professional, as a result.

Then came the tragic and avoidable death of Ruth Perry in 2023, a dedicated junior school head teacher who took her own life after a failed Ofsted inspection. One wonders how many other caring professionals have received such heartless injustice over the years. Career-ruining judgements based on relative minutiae in just one area of investigation landing on devoted and conscientious teachers without regard for the bigger picture within the school. How many have endured, as a result of similar treatment, prolonged ill-health, which may also have ultimately destroyed them? The facts of that particular event have been laid bare, are well-documented and are easy to find online. That this was a disturbing travesty of justice is the obvious conclusion to reach.

Before the end of the year, an inquest had concluded that the Ofsted inspection had been a contributary factor in Ruth Perry's death, which just sounds like a colossal understatement, to me.

Will that case change anything substantively? I doubt it. An essential ingredient of this flawed system is the political posturing that the government perceives as its potential appeal to voters. Give people what they want to know - is there local school any good or not - and preferably in just one word. For anyone prepared to scratch the surface of the judgement at all, the question remains the same. How do you judge between two words - one utterly damning and one not - that are separated by a possibly arbitrary decision to come down on one side or the other of a very fine dividing line. What leads to that final decision is by its very nature multi-faceted, yet, thumbs up and you survive, thumbs down and you fall. It involves knowingly choosing over-simplification over nuanced and complicated human interactions. It does not make sense, but it won't change. Your votes are too important to them.

8. Any Lessons to be Learnt?

If head teachers and other senior staff are to teach fewer lessons than previously, or even not at all, they are less likely to be able to empathise with the problems that teachers face on a daily basis. In my experience, that state of affairs was made worse where there was an additional distinct territorial separation between the classroom teachers and managers on the ground, who were, in theory at least, still there to support them. When the managers reach a stage where they can justify to themselves that the business of everyday education is no longer anything to do with them and that their remit is simply to make sure other people are doing their jobs properly, I think you have an unhealthy situation, which can only get worse. It is like saying there is no difference between a school and any other activity that has a cost attached to it. Most teachers see a fundamental difference. Their prime concern is with young people, their well-being and their progress. They do not view pupils as by-products of an economic system.

We had become aggrieved when our managers tried to escape from the action, as it appeared to us, by making existing curricular leaders into pastoral leaders, as well, thus creating an additional buffer layer to separate them from the children. This was not unheard of and we knew this was increasingly the pattern in other better performing schools. However, when the original managers in our case were replaced and changes were implemented by the new regime working in tandem with the local authority, the old ways of organising things were reinstated. The feeling that dealing with children was actually everyone on the site's responsibility was explicitly reinforced within the reorganised roles that characterised the new start.

A situation has got to be reached in which staff retention is more settled. Staff sickness, staff turnover and the quantity of supply teachers are often accurate indicators of the overall health of a school and certainly that is what I believed they should be looking at as a priority. The government purports to lay great emphasis on getting the right people into the classroom. In my time, it was a matter of keeping the right people at the school and not losing them to premature retirement, long term stress-related illness, onward recruitment by other, "easier" or more successful schools, or defection to commerce and industry.

On reflection, I believed that the importance of assessing your own capabilities as an individual within the institution was of paramount importance. At our school, the experience that we suffered was a salutary tale of some people apparently being promoted outside of their comfort zone. Nor was it just teachers and their managers that were in a quandary, but local government advisers and school governors, too. I never applied for a job that I thought that I might struggle with. I sometimes thought that I had been too tentative in this respect, but I felt that, if so, I had erred on the side of caution and never considered for a moment that I was out of my depth, in terms of any added responsibilities gained after I had been promoted.

The permanently appointed head teacher that helped clear up the original mess at our school in 1997 never appeared to have bitten off more than he could chew. He exuded a quiet self-confidence throughout the affair. There was no apparent self-doubt in his make-up, but when he left the school, his successor lacked the charisma that he possessed. So, the message would have to be, make sound judgements about your own capabilities at every stage of your career. There is no shame in settling for something less prestigious within hierarchies, where you can be purposeful and find a level of responsibility that is quite enough to be going on with.

I was pleased to have been around at a time when advances were made in the way that teachers and taught related to each other, namely, more positively in terms of personal interactions, less autocratically by teachers, less subserviently by pupils and more honestly than they had been in the past. However, this shift contributed some additional strains on the system because it conferred responsibilities, as well as rights, which some pupils (and their parents, unfortunately) could not always cope with in a grown-up way. *"What chance have these kids got with parents like that?"* became a common observation. Where there was no self-discipline to replace authoritarian discipline, it could sometimes leave a comparatively anarchic void. Nevertheless, I felt sure that most schools were actually healthier places to be in than they were when I was at school myself. Reason had rightly replaced the threat of corporal punishment as the most significant motivating factor for pupils. The removal of education by fear remains a magnificent legacy from the 1970s, for me.

My second decade as a teacher was the Eighties - the Thatcher era, of course. The effects of her policies were most harshly felt in the area that I came to in 1982. The closure of the mines and the dismantling of traditional heavy industries led to much hardship in communities like the one that I served in, and it all happened in a relatively short time. No sooner had the attendant free market "seeing-to" worked its way through the former nationalised industries than the formula was applied to the remaining public services, including education. The parameters put in place then still largely control how schools operate today with successive governments maintaining a similar approach ever since.

I am equally sure that there must have been steady overall progress and a general raising of standards in many areas since I left teaching and that the requirement for accountability and close scrutiny of what goes on in schools will have played a part in forging these improvements.

One such change for the better has been the lack of notice that is now required before an inspection can begin. In the earlier years, the announcement of a forthcoming visit heralded weeks of feverish activity, during which time staff forgot about the kids completely and became totally obsessed with passing the forthcoming Ofsted event. All the visible areas of the school were redecorated with pupils' work and other displays and mountains of paperwork were produced as evidence of their industrious intent, as they bent over backwards to persuade their visitors that their school was better than it was. It was often disingenuous and it was just a big game but one with serious consequences when it was lost.

We are surely likely to be benefiting these days also from the increased availability of data from other countries, for example, the Organisation of Economic Co-operation and Development's Programme for International Student

Assessment, or PISA tests. We are, perhaps, prepared to learn more readily than in the past from other national systems, where aspects of education services have developed that appear to have been having some success.

It is impossible to touch on equal educational opportunity without mentioning private education. If you can buy an advantage for your child in education that leads to further advantage in accessing higher education and the job market, there is no real equality of educational opportunity for those who can't afford to pay.

During the eleven years that I spent at my first school, I can only remember one pupil who we all thought was an obvious shoe-in candidate for Oxford or Cambridge. She was from a working-class background but the teachers were fully aware of her potential and encouraged her to go through the application process. She got four "A" grades at "A" level in the mid-1970s but was turned down by the top universities. We thought at the time that it was a travesty of justice. It also felt like we had been snubbed as an institution by an establishment that allegedly favoured the historic relationships between top universities and top public schools.

The defence of private education is that in a democracy that values individual freedoms and the rule of law above all else, health and education should be up for grabs, regardless of the impact on society as a whole. A democratically elected government with a mandate to do so could level the playing field a bit by charging private schools VAT, ending business rates relief and curtailing their charitable status, but any further moves would be likely to be regarded as a step too far. Any such changes would also be met with fierce resistance, of course, from those with a vested interest in maintaining the status quo. Yet, a situation which favours seven per cent of the population over everyone else, in what is otherwise generally thought of as a meritocracy, is blatantly not fair for the vast majority. Additionally, private pre-examination tutoring arrangements will continue to offer a helping hand to families that can afford them.

Improving neighbourhood comprehensives so that parents are happy to send their children there, rather than choosing to shell out large sums of money for private schooling that may not turn out to be all that sparkling in reality, remains the more attainable and realistic target.

Looking back, it became clear that the second half of my teaching career in school coincided with a time of enormous economic and social upheaval in the community that we served. What at times seemed like an incessant bombardment of problem behaviour that was inevitably linked to the wider issues beyond the gates wore me down in the end. I wished afterwards that I could have been more robust and for longer, but I had run out of steam.

I eventually admitted that even the management colleagues that I felt were so obviously getting it wrong had actually been dealt a tricky hand in the first place, though I don't think anyone would have recognised it as such at the time that we were all assembled to make something happen in our "new" co-educational school. It could not have been long before they realised that they were floundering. They looked for mutual support from other members of their increasingly beleaguered cabal and ultimately chose the wrong path for their own survival, alienating almost all of their colleagues in the process as they sought solutions that were unworkable and eventually outside of their power to control. That such groups in institutions look inwards to each other for solutions, rather than outwards and openly, is hardly unique.

The problems at this school had bubbled along for ages, but only parochially. They were probably of no immediate interest to anyone outside the neighbourhood, typifying the sort of communal chat about school that you would have found within catchment areas anywhere and at any time. When the affair that justifiably precipitated the school into the limelight became markedly more newsworthy, the local paper was quickly by-passed by sustained national media interest. We were catapulted into the national consciousness by a single incident and a cack-handed attempt to fix it. It was all too late. The cat was out of the bag.

The prelude to our low point had been a visit from the Queen. I could not help but feel frustrated by the contrasts that the royal visit had thrown up. Money was suddenly made available for cosmetics, when, apart from the already agreed new buildings, the amount spent on the children's education was been systematically reduced. The reigning monarch was rightly invited to commemorate the hundreds of years of continuous and successful education that had been provided prior to what was going on at that moment. Simultaneously and behind the mask, the school was actually on its knees as a place of learning, by then. No doubt, a lot of people would have enjoyed a cheery and memorable day. For that, a ridiculous amount of gloss was applied for weeks prior to the event, in the interest of a visit that was over in less than one hour. No amount of "putting on a good show" could hide what lurked beneath the surface for those that were left behind to face the days that followed. An appropriately warm welcome had been extended, and every consideration was given to making the day a success for all concerned. However, this was orchestrated by the same people who were overseeing the school's demise, in a process that took years, and was to the detriment of the many pupils who passed through it during that time.

The precipitating event concerning the girl who was unjustly excluded from school was symptomatic of the problems being faced, but it was not their cause. Neglect by officialdom was at the heart of it and was the common factor - from central government through its economic and education policies, from an Ofsted regime that allowed itself to be misled, from local government through its advisory and inspection service, who dithered when they should have listened to the workers on the "chalk face" and who failed to respond in time to avoid damage to the school, and from the school governors who made mistakes in their appointments and who failed to act once fault lines had become apparent. This was then compounded by poor decisions by those who had been appointed to manage, who increasingly turned their backs on their colleagues instead of embracing them in a joint enterprise. As a newly appointed management team, they had applied a prevalent ideology that intentionally blurred the previously distinct responsibilities of deputy heads. I thought from the off that the systems they had decided on were not fit for purpose in that place and at that time. The irretrievable rift that eventually developed between senior management and the rest of the staff was only partly due to this policy. The situation deteriorated further through a series of inadequate responses to the unremitting pressures that we faced.

The old coalfield communities will never again be singled out as they were in the 1980s and 1990s, when curtailing trade union power appeared to be at the top of the agenda. Lessons will surely have been learnt from the way those areas suffered after the implementation of the pit closure programme. Regardless of the rights and wrongs of the miners' strike, itself, the conflict and its aftermath had serious economic and social consequences. It seemed to me that a callous disdain was shown for the well-being of the people who lived there that lasted for years. It was not just the miners who lost out but all those who depended on them and especially their children. As teachers, our task was to pick up the pieces from the resulting fallout. As I discovered, that was certainly going to be a big ask.

Postscript

Two things have happened while the finishing touches were being made to the front cover of this book. Though both were good news, they also made me feel a little sheepish about my obvious earlier cynicism. Admittedly, they also took me a bit by surprise, yet I like to think I'm normally a glass half full sort of person.

Firstly, the incoming Labour government of 2024 announced its intention to remove VAT exemption and business rates charitable rates relief from private schools. There had been no justification for continuing to give a leg up to the already advantaged and I wholeheartedly welcomed the move.

Secondly, and in the wake of the Ruth Kelly tragedy, the government is rightly pushing ahead with the reform of Ofsted by scrapping the single headline judgements that have immediately followed school inspections.

Details of these changes are available to view on the government's own website. Both attracted considerable political attention and newspaper comment after the announcements were made.